The Role of the
Finance Director

Financial Times Management Briefings are happy to receive proposals from individuals who have expertise in the field of management education.

If you would like to discuss your ideas further, please contact Andrew Mould, Commissioning Editor.

Tel: 0171 447 2210
Fax: 0171 240 5771
e-mail: andrew.mould@ftmanagement.com

MANAGEMENT BRIEFINGS
FINANCE

The Role of the Finance Director

Second Edition

TERRY CARROLL

FINANCIAL TIMES
MANAGEMENT

FINANCIAL TIMES

MANAGEMENT

LONDON · SAN FRANCISCO
KUALA LUMPUR · JOHANNESBURG

*Financial Times Management delivers the knowledge,
skills and understanding that enable students,
managers and organisations to achieve their ambitions,
whatever their needs, wherever they are.*

London Office:
128 Long Acre, London WC2E 9AN
Tel: +44 (0)171 447 2000
Fax: +44 (0)171 240 5771
Website: www.ftmanagement.com

A Division of Financial Times Professional Limited

First published in Great Britain 1995
Second edition 1998

© Financial Times Professional Limited 1995, 1998

ISBN 0 273 63725 8

British Library Cataloguing in Publication Data
A CIP catalogue record for this book can be obtained from the British Library.

10 9 8 7 6 5 4 3 2 1

Typeset by Boyd Elliott Typesetting
Printed and bound in Great Britain

The Publishers' policy is to use paper manufactured from sustainable forests.

About the author

Terry Carroll is Managing Director of Hollins Consulting, where he specialises in strategic consultancy, executive recruitment, counselling and outplacement. In 1998, he qualified as a NLP practitioner. With 16 years financial services experience, up to chief executive and nine years as finance director of major organisations in both the private and public sector, Terry has also acquired experience across the whole general management spectrum, including as MD of a HR, recruitment and outplacement company.

After graduating in business studies from Bradford Management Centre, he followed a career in finance. He has been responsible for strategic planning, information systems, treasury and risk management, human resources, sales and quality. His public sector experience includes three years as director of the largest NHS trust in the UK and several years as chairman or director of Inner City Projects.

As a non-executive director, Terry's specialist areas are strategy, treasury, risk and corporate governance. He has written many articles and publications and is an experienced conference presenter on these topics, together with finance and personal development. In 1998, he will complete a further book on risk management. He is a Chartered Accountant, Corporate Treasurer, Chartered Banker and former Member of the London Stock Exchange.

In his spare time, he plays golf, tennis and bridge, writes poetry and music. He is currently working on an allegorical novel and a cello concerto. Married to Heather Summers, a HR and training consultant, they have two sons and one daughter.

For further information, contact:

Terry Carroll FCA, FCT, FCIB, MIMgt
Managing Director
Hollins Consulting
Hollins House
Bishop Thornton
Harrogate HG3 3JZ

Tel/fax: (01765) 620643
Mobile: (0374) 973721

Contents

Foreword

During the research and preparation of both editions, I spoke to or corresponded with many people, especially chairmen, chief executives, managing directors and finance directors of organisations in both the private and public sectors. Apart from being grateful for the many contributions, I was particularly delighted at the continuing high degree of accord with my own views on the rapidly developing finance director's role, as captured in the following pages.

It is customary for someone who is well-known or influential and who has relevant knowledge to write a short foreword. In this case, however, I feel that the contributions of three eminent business leaders continue to summarise the views of many.

Sir Rocco Forte values good management, excellent technical skills and the ability to relate to key influencers inside and outside the organisation:

The key qualities I look for in a finance director are the following:

- In a Plc, relationships with the investment community and ability to obtain their confidence;

- A clear understanding of all the competencies relating to the role i.e. treasury, tax, financial control;

- A good understanding of management techniques, he himself has to manage teams both directly and in a functional capacity;

- An ability to understand what makes the business tick, and which are the levers that can be pulled;

- A committed member of the top management team who will take ownership of, and responsibility for, the figures that make up the financial results, not just report them.

The Hon. Sir Rocco Forte, 1995.

Sir William Purves and Sir Nicholas Goodison have both served at the helm of major banking corporations, operating in complex global markets. Every competitive organisation needs to take account of global influences, whether or not they are operating or selling overseas. All the financial markets of the world are dominated by global trading, especially in foreign exchange and derivatives. The latter are also increasingly driving the direction of the cash markets in money and commodities. If anyone is aware of the effects of this growing complexity on modern organisations, it is these two eminent bankers.

Sir Nicholas focuses on the key factors of internationalisation, escalating risk and the effects of technology and innovation in driving change. He also notes the importance of looking after the interests of shareholders (one of the groups of stakeholders in organisations):

> The role of the finance director in a major corporation today is more complex than in the past and of crucial importance. The normal duties relating to financial soundness, control, strategy, reporting and the external presentation of financial matters, have been greatly increased by the need for effective risk management in an increasingly competitive and fast-moving world. The internationalisation of business, and the constant change brought about in financial markets by innovation and technology, increase the degree of risk analysis and risk control. The finance director has duties which go beyond management, acting as a monitor of a company's financial performance on behalf of shareholders: an able finance director can be of inestimable help to the chairman of a company in this role.
>
> **Sir Nicholas Goodison, 1995.**

Sir William is concerned that the FD should also be able to provide information to inform management decisions related to other stakeholders, including customers and suppliers. The broad concept of stakeholders is one which puts all organisations on a common footing. In particular, all organisations have customers and need to take account of public interest.

As well as technical skills, Sir William looks for a range of personal qualities, an understanding of the business and the ability to use technology effectively to provide the data to inform management decisions:

In a large international financial services group the finance director must of course have excellent technical skills in finance and accounting. However these are of limited use if he or she does not also have a deep understanding of the business of the group and the markets in which it operates. Objectivity, independence and intellectual honesty are personal qualities which are needed in order that he can give management a clear unbiased view of financial performance and of investment/disinvestment decisions. Modern technology facilitates the cost effective storage of large quantities of data. Today, the finance director should strive to give his company a competitive edge by developing financial information systems which transform this data into relevant information for management decisions about lines of business, products, customers and suppliers, as well as about investment projects and risk assessment.

Sir William Purves, 1995.

It is reassuring but not surprising to find that these eminent businessmen also recognise the rapidly evolving breadth and complexity of the role of the finance director. This book covers many different aspects of the role as well as those referred to in this foreword. It should confirm to all readers that the challenge of maximising the contribution made by the FD requires both organisations and FDs to re-examine the role and cast aside the assumptions of the past.

Preface

When I set out to write the first edition of this book, I had several objectives. First, the book should not be a textbook on a potentially dry subject, but should be easy for all readers to use. It was not written just for finance directors, but for anyone who came into contact with the role. I never intended it to be prescriptive, but hoped it would be thought provoking and challenging.

The book unashamedly attempts to be more 'right-brained' in discussing what is seen largely as a 'left-brained' role, usually held by accountants trained in logical, precise thinking. In the 21st century a more holistic thinking and management style will be encouraged.

While every management decision has financial consequences, it is the decision and the holistic processes which lead to it which is important. Shared, informed, decisions which take into account the customer, the strategy, the risks, the people, processes and systems necessary to effect them, as well as the financial consequences, are the way forward. The FD of the future should be a team player, able to engage in this holistic thinking process, rather than a 'pursekeeper' who holds the power of veto.

The first edition attempted to address all the likely aspects of the role, in a way which set it in the future, rather than the present or the past. Change will be continuous, affecting society, industry and individual organisations, just as much as it affects the people who give them their being. Managing for the *status quo* will no longer be an option. Many issues likely to arise were therefore covered in passing. Most are still relevant, but new ones will emerge, priorities will change and the role of the finance director will continue to evolve. This second edition broadens some of the aspects of the role, addresses several major new issues and expands on much of the earlier thinking.

There are three particular issues (the year 2000 problem, the single currency and the use of derivatives) and three aspects of the role (corporate governance, information systems and risk), which have assumed even greater prominence during the last two years. These will be covered fully in this edition, with the role of the information manager now meriting its own chapter. The author is also engaged on another project under the working title *Risk for Directors* to cover what has at last become a priority.

The world changes so fast that within weeks of the first edition being published, two of the three contributors to the foreword had seen their companies merged. Nevertheless, the views of Lord Forte, Sir Nicholas Goodison and Sir William Purves remain relevant and they themselves are still widely respected for their business achievements. In this edition, some new quotations have been added, and some deleted.

I believe language is important for breaking down gender stereotypes, but I acknowledge that many people find it easier to write using the male gender. I am quite sure that this does not indicate prejudice in any way. The openness of mind demonstrated in the quotations is testimony to a new, flexible and adaptable approach across a range of organisations. My own view is that right-brain skills will come to be increasingly valued in both the management and culture of organisations, and my own text is written without reference to gender.

I have been much encouraged by the general response to the first edition. Although I felt it was a book which needed writing, I never dreamt it would become a 'best-seller'. For that I am indebted to my new publisher, Financial Times Management. Many people have contacted me to say they have read the book. Fortunately no-one so far has disagreed with its main themes. Indeed, several have said that the greater emphasis on people is to be welcomed, especially in the professional Institutes.

After preparing this substantially revised text, I was able to read the excellent book by Price Waterhouse's team (1997), based on their worldwide survey of CFOs. Once again, I was reassured by the high degree of convergence with the present text. Indeed, I would only raise two points of departure: the importance of emphasising 'stakeholders' rather than shareholders; and that even as it was published, the year 2000 problem had reached critical proportions. It would have been useful to know how many of the CFOs they spoke to were even aware of the problem, let alone had taken account of it. The treatment in this book is in much starker terms!

Whether you are a new or previous reader, I sincerely hope you enjoy reading this book and will continue to dip into it for years to come.

Acknowledgements

In the first edition, there were many people to thank for their help and co-operation. Many directors took the time and trouble to supply thoughts and quotations. Most were highly relevant and topical; some remain 'ahead of the game'.

Finally, since the first edition and with a change of publisher, I would not wish to lose sight of the encouragement and support given by Glyn Jones in the early days. Without this and the happiness I have found with my lovely, talented life partner, Heather Summers (a constant source of original ideas), this and the new projects on which I am working might have remained a dream.

1

Introduction

The role of the finance director (FD), chief finance officer (CFO), or its equivalent, is central to the integrity, security, efficiency, viability, development and success of all organisations. That role is continually evolving. While many may still have a somewhat traditional view that the holder is either the bookkeeper or 'super accountant', forward thinking organisations and indeed finance directors are taking the role into aspects that would have been unthought of in the 1950s.

This book is about the evolving role of the FD. While many of the core aspects may remain the same, the role and how it is performed will have to change and become more flexible in much the same way as organisations. While many of the matters discussed in this book relate to 'industrial' or 'corporate' FDs or CFOs, the principles and the general approach are applicable to any environment and sector. Public sector organisations, including the civil service, are being run in a more businesslike manner. Many FDs transferred to the public sector in the 1990s, especially the NHS, and took best commercial practice with them.

This is not to say that the traffic is all one way. Some public sector approaches relating to values, equality and environment – the more caring aspects – are also being adopted by far-sighted companies. All organisations have customers, stakeholders, finances and interaction with the public. It may be assumed by some that not all of this book is relevant to the FDs of small medium enterprises (SMEs). With one or two obvious exceptions, such as where the organisation is unitary, not acquisitive, has no overseas trade or exposure, this may be true. In general, however, the text is particularly important to SMEs, for it is in these organisations that the broad responsibilities may fall on one individual, who may not even have board status. The requirements remain largely the same, including the need to define clearly the roles and responsibilities of all the executives and capture them in a procedures manual, or similar.

Leader, team player

In the modern organisation, the FD should be expected to be an experienced, skilful general manager, a leader and a team player, as well as performing the specialist duties which have become associated with the role. As you will see, these duties are now potentially widespread. For all these reasons, organisations should not be content simply to appoint an excellent accountant. The finance function is potentially an expensive overhead unless the modern FD and the finance team can play an active part in all the relevant management processes of the organisation. This means moving away from the traditional 'number-crunching' routine, ensuring that the systems are in place to provide the information managers need as and when it is needed, and providing advice, guidance and support as appropriate.

Qualifications

Every FD should have an appropriate professional qualification. There is a lively debate on what this should be. Most would say the FD should hold a qualification of one of the six accountancy bodies recognised by the Consultative Committee of Accountancy Bodies (CCAB). Nevertheless, some famous and successful 'non-accountants' have been FDs. The most notable was Archie Norman when he was FD of Kingfisher PLC. Although highly successful in the role, Archie possessed 'only' a Harvard MBA and a spell at the consultants McKinseys to back up his appointment to high office! History shows this was no bar to his success, especially when he was appointed chief executive of Asda.

My mind is open on the point. The main advantage of qualified accountants is that they are 'steeped' in the financial aspects that really matter. The downside is that accountants do not always make good strategists or people managers. This is changing as organisations look increasingly for visionary management, intuition, creativity, holistic thinking and other right-brained characteristics. Some are finding these (though not exclusively) in a growing number of women finance directors. This is particularly true in the public sector. There is no doubt that a business qualification of some sort, such as MBA, DMA, DBS, etc. would be an advantage for the broader demands.

Right brain skills

As Dr Harry Alder says in *The Right Brain Manager*:

> Companies have to start making way for a new breed of free-thinking executives, whatever the present structure and prevailing culture. Management development programmes have to incorporate right-brain techniques for problem-solving, time management and other managerial responsibilities. (Alder, 1993).

Henry Mintzberg also makes the case:

> One fact recurs repeatedly in all of this research: the key managerial processes are enormously complex and mysterious. . .drawing on the vaguest of information and using the least articulated mental processes. These processes seem to be

> more relational and holistic than ordered and sequential, and more intuitive than intellectual; they seem to be most characteristic of right-hemispheric activity. (Mintzberg, 1973).

By now you will realise that this is neither a text book, nor a traditional treatise on financial and management accounting. Leading edge organisations are changing in response to the apparent 'chaos' in their business environment. I have found the traditionalist view too restrictive. Of course a FD must be expected to lead the accounting and control processes of the organisation, but not as a restraint on flexibility, with information conveyed in a dry, incomprehensible set of statistics. The FD should be a facilitator of financial understanding; an internal consultant to managers held accountable for their performance. In addition, as right hand to the chairman, chief executive or MD, a key player in the top team and increasingly responsible for strategic planning, the successful FD should be expected to display a broader range of managerial and interpersonal skills. You will find this thread woven throughout the book.

A member of the board

While using the title finance director (FD), this book relates to the most senior financial role in the organisation. Although they may carry the title chief financial officer, general manager finance, financial controller, financial manager, chief accountant or similar, the most senior finance person should always have a seat on the board of directors or equivalent body. The role is so important that the FD or equivalent should be accountable to the board. By virtue of being a member of the board, the FD is better able to act with impartiality, in the best interests of the organisation. Although in small organisations, the chief executive, managing director, sole owner, etc. may assume this role, it is in the best interests of the organisation and its viability and success for the role to be separated as soon as it is practically and financially possible.

It is inequitable and unrealistic to charge a senior financial officer with the responsibilities of a director without the designation. It is difficult to see how such a person could be accountable to the board for their actions otherwise. Although all directors are collectively and individually responsible for the governance of the organisation, the finance director has special responsibilities which can only be delegated upwards. The FD is the person responsible for objectively making the board aware of the financial consequences of strategy or business decisions. FDs must be impartial, with no axe to grind. They must therefore be equal participants in the process.

The need for change

Every director is also a general manager and the FD is no exception. As managers, they are not only responsible for managing the systems, processes and resources of finance. Every FD is responsible for people and no-one should be able to sustain that role in the modern organisation without an understanding of good management practice. Although accountants do not always make good managers of people, there is no excuse for abdicating the role or not at least understanding the principles of good management.

We now realise that change is a constant factor and that organisations must continually evolve in order to remain competitive or viable. Teamwork is the current creed. The FD cannot remain aloof from colleagues, passing down tablets of stone or decreeing what can or cannot be spent. The controlling role of the past must now be replaced with a facilitating approach. The response should not be 'we can't do that' but rather 'here are the options open to us and the financial and business consequences of each.'

A good FD will no longer be the Pythonesque accountant (narrow of training and outlook), but must now possess and display managerial skills and leadership qualities, together with an ability to think strategically and communicate clearly.

The FD is a key officer, manager and professional in any organisation. It would not be unusual for this role to be seen as the third most important, after the chairman and chief executive/managing director. However, if this is the case, there should be a good partnership and dialogue between the FD and the marketing director, so that the former helps to meet customers' needs, rather than acts as a brake on the organisation's prosperity. FDs are not exempt from the need to operate in a quality way – after all, everyone in the organisation is a customer of the FD, even if only their wages are involved. Furthermore, with a low inflation economy for the foreseeable future, FDs are having to bend the traditional target rates of return on capital from a norm of fifteen to twenty per cent (giving real returns of fifteen per cent or so), otherwise competitiveness, output, development and employment in the UK will decline.

It is also increasingly the case that the FD has responsibility for information systems and treasury. The three new major issues covered in this edition (Year 2000, EMU and Derivatives) all fall within these aspects. Truly a new breed is required to manage these complexities. This does not make the present incumbent redundant. We now live in a learning society. For those who wish to remain in post, a constant hunger for knowledge will stand them in good stead, personally and professionally.

All in all, therefore, plenty of challenges face today's FD. Adaptability and flexibility will be key. The dinosaurs will become extinct. The process of change has accelerated in the last few years. Nevertheless, while certain aspects of the core role should remain unchanged (especially the governance aspects), it is possible to trace a pattern of evolution of the role in any industry, and indeed the UK and elsewhere, since the 1960s.

2

The role and functions of the finance director

The changing role

New pressures are transforming the finance directors of British companies from aloof and authoritarian figures into executives with different abilities and approaches – and, in the process, raising questions about the traditional dominance of the job by accountants. One set of pressures is the shifting balance from finance director as controller to businessman, from scorekeeper to commercial operator. Where once there was a special fiefdom, there are signs that barriers between finance and other parts of the business are breaking down. The finance director is becoming a team player, more a general manager than a technical expert. (Sir Geoffrey Owen, 1995, former editor *Financial Times*).

The changing role of the FD is as much as anything a function of the changing corporate environment in which the organisation and the FD operate. The private sector cannot ignore the effects of globalisation and 'Europeanisation'. We now live and work in a 'knowledge society' where information is the key to competitive advantage. No serious player can afford to be less than a quality player. Successful companies in the future will be those which are expert in information and quality management, but also have a synergistic 'team' of people with a breadth of skills and experience: flexible, adaptable, innovative and entrepreneurial, with a clear mission and goals but with management processes capable of responding to rapid and continual change. The portfolio of the FD will include acknowledged technical skills, but also strategic, commercial, people management and interpersonal skills.

All sectors

This manifesto is not just for the private sector. Most of this report is of direct relevance to all FDs, wherever they are working. FDs in the public sector will be increasingly influenced by attitudes and practices in the private sector, for a number of reasons.

- A growing number of FDs will migrate between sectors.

- The public sector will need to import more private sector or commercial practices, as public funds become tighter and the need grows to demonstrate value for money and still deliver the service.

- There will be a growth of partnerships with the private sector – the Private Finance Initiative will be a major influence in this.

- There will be a growing demand to market test non-core services (and even core services in some cases); and

- In-house business cases will need to be phrased in the same commercial terms as outside tenders.

Strategic and commercial role

> Essentially he must be a key member of the business team contributing fully to strategy formulation and carrying out his financial duties...In relation to his financial responsibility pre-eminent would be financial controls, monitoring and reporting of the highest standards with good quality analysis of events past, present and in particular future. His judgements of future issues should essentially be commercial rather than accountancy based and in most organisations he must represent something of the conscience of the business in matters ethical. . .If the organisation is a quoted business then his role with the city and the advice he gives is of key importance. (Murray Stuart, 1995, Chairman, Scottish Power plc).

> Clearly the finance director is responsible for the traditional areas such as the company's financial and management reporting and its treasury operations together with, in many cases, internal audit and information technology. Each of these is a growing art or science in its own right and, were the job to stop there, it would be a challenging one. But in addition the finance director is very often the only main board executive director, apart from the chief executive, whose remit extends across all the divisional boundaries. Therefore there is a key role to be played in developing corporate strategy, which is probably of greater added value than the more traditional aspects of the finance director's job. (James Loudon, 1995, Treasurer, Scottish Hydro-Electric plc).

Woven through these different views are a number of commonalities: the role is changing; it is becoming more complex and broader; the traditional functions have been augmented by strategy, risk management and a more commercial approach; personal and management skills are now critical to membership of the 'team'; but the FD is still regarded as seated with the chief executive in the management team and the chairman in the board.

Yet, while these shared views indicate development and change, the business environment, society and the organisation are experiencing change at an even faster rate. The challenge for tomorrow's FD is to keep up with that speed of change and still ensure that the organisation has the information to understand how it is performing against its plan and its competitors.

Furthermore, the finance function will increasingly be seen as an overhead in the disaggregated organisation, needing to justify its existence. Governance and stewardship will be mandatory but the information is needed 'real-time' on managers' desks, through an interactive network. The FD will increasingly become an internal consultant providing advice, guidance and support to the organisation and managing a tightly defined group of specialist functions including strategic planning, tax, treasury, statutory and regulatory reporting, accounting and control, financial services, and so on. Some of these will increasingly be outsourced. In the future slim and efficient corporate head office, quality will supersede quantity in the finance function and value for money will be paramount as long as the status and the viability of the organisation remain intact.

Stakeholders and short-termism

In the corporate sector, the prime objective of a company should be to maximise stakeholder value over the long term. Many would say this would be shareholder value in relation to quoted companies. This is discussed elsewhere. No organisation can afford to overlook any of its five key stakeholders: its customers, suppliers, owners, employees, and, increasingly the public at large and in the immediate community. It is interesting to reflect on differing attitudes elsewhere. Organisations worldwide now recognise the importance of valuing, empowering and involving their employees. While this is common currency, in Japan the customer is first and longer term objectives prevail. Investors know that the Japanese are world masters at putting the customer first. In the US, corporations are not ashamed to trumpet their investment in and sponsorship of the community. This is now often reflected and valued in corporate brands. In the UK we are still reticent about this.

These different interests are reflected in the way this book has been written. If, for example, we take just one aspect: many experts and industrialists claim that maximisation of long term shareholder value is the prime objective of a quoted company and that the share price represents the net present value of the future stream of earnings. Yet, 'short-termism' prevails in the UK. Share prices are volatile and react strongly to an extraordinary profits forecast or a warning of performance shortfall. This probably inhibits longer term investment (with some exceptions). Furthermore, many analysts and observers still refer to the Price/Earnings (P/E) ratio as an indicator of relative value. In the US and the UK, cashflow has become the most important indicator to watch. It is lack of cash that bankrupts companies rather than lack of capital. Even the accountancy bodies now regard the P/E multiple as being of dubious value. This is also discussed later.

Performance measurement

As well as reconciling the cash based performance with the profit based picture, there is an increasing desire not to see the corporation in terms of tightly defined accounting periods. There are a number of reasons for this. Accounting practices, including depreciation and other non-cash factors, can make the monthly or annual financial performance seem to bear no relation to the business performance. The financial information is by definition historical. Where the information is complex, or the systems are inadequate to the task, it can also be meaningless, so why waste the effort collecting, digesting and regurgitating it? Good managers should have their own performance information at their fingertips. By the time the board sits down, they should not only know what happened last month, the reasons why and the action they have already taken to rectify the situation, but also the likely performance for this month and next month – 'realtime'.

As a management accountant, the FD would previously have provided only financial information for present performance and future projection. Now, in the era of the balanced scorecard, value management and other approaches, and with change being constant, a wider digest of information is required. Hence the growing trend for FDs to take responsibility for all management information and the systems which supply it. Thereby, they become a supplier to every internal customer.

Strategic planning

Strategic planning is an annual exercise for those organisations which do it. This should set the parameters for performance for the planning period, but also needs to be a live, evolving document. It will include broad business as well as financial targets, but how many monthly reports reflect broad performance measurement against the plan, let alone the changing outlook for an evolving plan? The way financial information is presented can be meaningless and impenetrable to management and wholly out of relation to the actual day-to-day performance they are seeing.

Balancing old and new skills

There is a need for understanding and co-operation between the members of the top team. If the FD is seen first and foremost as a general manager, outward facing, walking the shop, relating easily to the organisation at large, the battle may be half won. There is a need to balance new skills with old skills. Accounting may be a legal requirement, but many of the old, labour-intensive, historical practices are an overhead the organisation can no longer afford. Markets can change and customers be lost in less time than it takes to produce the monthly accounts.

Whether quoted or private or even in the public or 'non-profit' sectors, the challenges for the FD are growing: to develop as a broad manager and team player as well as cope with the breadth and pace of change. A growing number of commentators now see the need for broader experience and broader based qualifications for the FD. Writing when he was Managing Director of NBS (one of the leading headhunters in the UK), David Timson said:

> my conclusion was that it would be no surprise if, in the not too distant future, finance directors would need to be both qualified accountants and MBAs and a lot of other things as well....It is not too far fetched to expect many companies to begin listing (the Diploma of the Association of Corporate Treasurers) as a prerequisite for finance directors positions.... (Timson, 1995).

It could be argued that accountants have had too much power in UK industry. Germany and the US have been the two major economies in the world in the 20th century (together with Japan). The former has more engineers than accountants leading its industry. The latter has more marketeers. The future FD will need to be more of a general manager with sound financial instincts and less of an accountant.

The successful FD of the future will need modern skills – a visionary, steeped in quality management; a leader who empowers teams; an information manager with a good understanding of what motivates customers; and, above all, a strategist. All these and many other skills will still need to be tempered with an instinct for corporate governance – and an eye for what is right, to be used where the organisation's mission, viability, legality, values or ethics are at risk.

I do not propose to list the functional roles of the FD. Certain of them will always be core, but outside these they will evolve to match the individual to the organisation's needs. Reference is made later in this chapter to wide ranging surveys of the components. Many aspects of the role have evolved since the 1950s, especially as society, the economic world and companies' needs and modus operandi have evolved.

Evolution of the FD's role

The 1960s

In the 1960s, industry discovered corporate planning. This involved, among other things, appraising the strengths and weaknesses of the company and the opportunities and threats in its environment (SWOT analysis). Operations research (OR) came into vogue and companies looked at themselves in more financial and numerical detail than ever before. Companies organised themselves in a deliberate way and as well as manpower planning for the future, the art of general management began to appear with formal roles and responsibilities drawn up. There were far fewer FDs than now, but the challenges facing them began to go well beyond the bookkeeping and annual accounts. Leading companies diversified more, by development and acquisition (there was also the start of rationalisation and secular decline of staple industries). All of these changes required a growing involvement from the FD, to quantify the consequences, support the developments, input to project costings and financially appraise the options. The science of costing developed (e.g. standard costing and budgetary control) although the art of costing (zero-based, activity based, etc.) took much longer to arrive.

The 1970s

The 1970s saw the arrival of portfolio management and the Boston matrix (developed by the Boston Consulting Group). The management consultancy industry was established and grew rapidly taking the lead from McKinsey and others. It was not unusual for recently qualified accountants to seek a short cut to the FD's office, through a spell in a leading consultancy. Market share and the importance of cash management came to the fore. More quantification and analysis were needed. Oil prices zoomed and inflation exploded. The economy and the stock market boomed, slumped and boomed again. Historic accounting was not enough and various methods of inflation accounting were proposed. Exposure drafts and statements of standard accounting practice were produced at regular frequencies.

As well as grappling with the complexities of accounting (the true and fair view), corporate FDs found themselves managing shareholders' expectations as personal equity holdings declined (to be replaced by unit trusts) and institutional shareholdings grew. It was the era when the pension fund came to the fore and every company had to plan not only to provide for the contributions but also to account correctly. Personal and corporate tax became more complex, especially as companies came up with innovative ways to reward their most valuable employees (share options, cars, loans, etc.) including of course the FD. The brief of the FD now ranged from planner to accountant, company secretary to auditor, information systems manager to property manager, tax to remunerations and pensions manager. Meanwhile, corporate treasury was on the move! Some well-known names (such as Rowntrees speculating in cocoa) contrived new ways to make and lose money in e.g. the futures market.

The 1980s

Many of the changes in the 1980s really occurred towards the end of the decade, although the radical Tory government drove through a huge legislative programme. This not only reduced tax rates and delivered more choice and freedom to individuals and companies, but also sold most of the 'family silver' in the biggest privatisation programme in the world.

The same 'leaders' of the 1960s now realised that diversification may have gone too far; the expected financial returns had not materialised and they had lost sight of the core business, becoming cumbersome and unwieldy in the process. Management and leveraged buyouts were in vogue, adding a whole new raft of companies to the stock market until eventually it became choked with equity. Equities were overvalued, interest rates were edging up, the longer term economic prospects looked gloomy and the world's markets collapsed in October 1987. Shortly afterwards, confidence in property evaporated as well. Companies found funding more difficult and their assets had fallen in value. Liquidation and rationalisation followed (and on into the 1990s). The FD now had to plan and account for huge redundancy and rationalisation programmes.

Information technology change was rapid. The FD had to be computer literate. Downsizing of companies was paralleled by downsizing of computing in the age of the PC. Companies no longer needed huge mainframes, the FD got less paper, but was able to deliver more real time information to the manager's desk through an intelligent terminal. Spreadsheet packages provided powerful modelling capability and strategic decisions could be made rapidly. With automation and robotics, the development time for new products shortened dramatically, enabling competitive advantage. Unfortunately, competitors were in the same position and entry barriers came down. The need was for sustainable advantage through differentiation by exponential improvement in quality. Rate of return was superseded by payback where the target period shortened to two years or less.

The FD now had to add critical success factors to key performance indicators in the jargon of measurement. This change carried across all sectors, as did the growing preoccupation with total quality management (TQM) and customer care. It was the start of the globalisation of markets and all senior managers had to be aware and capable of working with new cultures. Japanese overseas investment and competition in a growing range of markets substantially sharpened the better companies, while many of the worse started to go to the wall or shrank back into a niche. America was not alone in studying and implementing Japanese management and work practices, including the methods of Deming (the father of TQM), who was himself an American.

Working with new cultures was growing inside companies. The growing preoccupation with Quality and Excellence brought into sharp relief the culture and values of the organisation. Those who could not change or adapt would shortly join the growing army of managers in the dole queues. As the 1990s have shown, FDs and accountants are not immune and a professional qualification is no longer a meal ticket.

The 1990s

And so into the 1990s – the decade of quality, process re-engineering and chaos management. 500,000 white collar workers are estimated to have lost their jobs in the recession. Employment of men and full timers fell, while part-timers, especially women, have grown in number and proportion. There are now more women than men in employment in the UK economy. Nobody's job is secure, not even the FD. Companies have downsized dramatically and reduced job security in the process. In 1988, the CBI estimated that by 1995, four million people would be working from home (good news for the FD as overheads decline). While some put the figure as low as 2.5 million now, more and more people work on a subcontract or consultancy basis.

Decentralisation has led to slimming down of the head office function. More production is bought in from overseas at lower cost. More support functions are contracted out in the second leaf of Charles Handy's 'Shamrock organisation'. (Handy, 1989). The portfolio career is here to stay, despite the dramatically improved employment prospects for those who did not retire completely during and following the recession. More 'grey hairs' are being recruited back, partly as a result of shortages of skills and partly because younger managers have not yet been through the curve. Many of these sages may only be used to bridge the gap, as mentors, or increasingly on a consultancy basis, to suit the rapidly evolving global economy.

Relationship management and strategic partnerships and alliances are the order of the day. For quoted companies, shareholder value is the focus, but growing short termism has produced frequent changes of strategy and direction, particularly as companies seek to appease their institutional investors. Reorganisation, rationalisation and management shakeups have accelerated. Loyalty has declined on both sides. Rewards, especially for top FDs, have grown, but neither employers nor employees seem tied to a long term relationship.

Share options and top executives' pay have come under the microscope of public opinion. The general public, fed by the press, has the corporation and its public behaviour and accountability under closer scrutiny. The remuneration of executives has entered the politic arena and has become part of the manifesto that some would like to incorporate in a growing governance role for institutional fund managers, now controlling a collective 2/3 of major quoted companies' equity while their attendance at AGMs and overt influence on company policy and governance remains scant.

Europe

The European dimension has not only brought greater complexity to the FD's role through legislation and regulation which cannot be ignored, but also wider markets to compete in on equal terms and the inevitability of a single currency which very few understand and not many are trying to explain. The collapse of the Soviet bloc has also opened up new markets, but once they have bought the capital goods and infrastructure of Western capitalism, these may prove to be more of a competitive threat than an opportunity (especially on cost, unless they join the high cost EC). The 'tiger' economies ebb and flow, creating even greater instability in the global economy.

Green issues prevail and environmental consequences cannot be ignored. Teamwork, leadership, empowerment, innovation and intrapreneurship are the currencies of visionary companies. The quality of management decisions is paramount. The FD now truly needs to be a people manager, a communicator and a general manager. Every bit as much as the managing director, he or she must have an understanding and an insight into the roles and specialities of the other senior managers, with whom they are partners in the success or failure of the enterprise.

Anyone who has lived or worked through the last 30 years must have seen some of this change, only a fraction of which is captured above. Every change, every business decision has risks attached and financial consequences. Not only has the role of the FD become immensely more complex in this period, but also it is no longer the case that the FD will 'do the numbers bit' and let the rest of the team manage their own roles in the implementation. FDs are key players. Their strategic leadership, involvement, style, communication skills, resilience, adaptability and general management skills with both peers and subordinates are now critical.

Key aspects of the finance director's role

In November 1993, the Financial Executives Group of the Board for Chartered Accountants in Business published its report on *The Changing Role of the Finance Director*. (Owen and Able, 1993). Among its findings, it concluded that 'the job of Finance Director is becoming more complex and more demanding' and that 'the broadening of the finance director's role is focusing attention on the appropriate training and experience for the job'. Five years later, the responsibilities are still growing, especially in SMEs.

The table below indicates growing complexity:

Table 2.1
Responsibility of finance departments; relative importance; change in last five years.

Activity	Responsibility	High/medium importance	Up in the previous 5 years
Mgt accounting	97	95	50
Taxation	87	76	30
Treasury	83	75	42
Acquisitions	75	53	26
Strat planning	71	69	42
Insurance	71	60	15
IT	68	63	43
Pensions	65	56	26
Internal audit	60	43	21
Legal affairs	58	47	13
Investor relations	50	46	27
Property	47	29	10

(*Source: The Changing Role of the Finance Director*. Owen and Able, 1993.)

This picture is changing steadily. In a later survey by the London Business School, sponsored by Egon Zehnder International (1997), while strategic planning (54%), investor relations (47%), treasury and tax (23%) are still rated among the top priorities by significant proportions, pensions was selected by 0% (but was rated among the lowest priorities by 61%) and corporate governance by only 9% (but low by 51%). Meanwhile, corporate finance (49%), team management (33%) and risk management (17%), have become major preoccupations. In five years time, the top three competences seen as needed by CFOs are: strategic leadership (65%); team building (52%); and communication (45%).

Since the first edition, the present text has increased in length by fifty per cent, simply to absorb all the aspects and challenges for all FDs.

3

The FD in different industries and sectors

> He who has his thumb on the purse has the power. (Otto von Bismarck).

The vast majority of FDs in the UK are in companies in the private sector; all these should be preoccupied with stakeholder management. This is most true in the public sector. Public opinion is becoming increasingly important to organisations in the public eye. Issues such as the environment and remuneration of top people have provoked a growing public reaction, widely reported in the media. The various Citizens' Charter initiatives and a growing public focus on quality, sensitised by quality organisations and strengthened by consumer selectivity in the high street (particularly matching quality and value for money), have led organisations to become more aware of their impact on a wider population. Everybody is a potential or actual customer. It is no longer sufficient to focus on your existing customers. Even people who might never buy your products can affect your market perception. Word of mouth is still the most powerful marketing tool – for or against you.

While this book focuses mainly on the private sector, most of the messages for the FD or equivalent are equally relevant to the public sector or non-profit organisations (e.g. charities). Company directors may wish to skip this chapter, but if not will, I hope, find something of value in the next few pages. In particular, an increasing number of people, including FDs, are migrating between the private and public sectors. In her book *How To Be Headhunted* Yvonne Sarch refers to the increasing attractiveness of candidates who have both private and public sector experience. (Sarch, 1991). Furthermore, in the last few years, many senior executives have been recruited into the public sector, for example as FDs of NHS hospital trusts.

This chapter gives a brief overview of some factors which might influence the FD's role in non-profit making organisations. However, the growing importance of the Private Finance Initiative (PFI), means an increasing number of public/private sector partnerships. Together with the pragmatic recognition by the new Labour government that the private sector will become more involved in 'public' projects, because of a shrinking public purse, there is value in leaders from both sectors understanding how the 'other half' lives.

The non-profit organisation

What happens when you do not have the objective of making a profit? How do you motivate yourself and what are your goals? Peter Drucker asks 'What is the bottom line when there is no bottom line?' (Drucker, 1990). He proposes that the mission comes first.

In my experience, the one consistent focus is value for money (frequently abbreviated to VFM). If you are running a hospital trust, a local authority or similar organisation, you are expected to account to your funders (taxpayers, ratepayers, government, etc.) how you spend the money. Cost-efficiency is consistently stated as 'growing value for money'. A charity will be expected to show that the proportion of funds distributed to causes is as high as possible in relation to the administration costs of running that charity. A school will be expected to show improving performance in league tables of academic results.

Altruism is an overused word but many people have transferred into public sector care organisations because they believe they can apply their skills to generate a meaningful contribution to society (e.g. more patients treated for the same money). Whatever the reasons for someone arriving in the FD's office (or equivalent) in a non-profit organisation there is increasing convergence with the private sector. Whether it is best commercial practice or governance, accounting standards or benchmarking, an increasing range of skills and experience are relevant in all FDs' roles.

Managing finance in the non-profit organisation

In the non-profit organisation (NPO) there is no profit, but there is a series of 'bottom lines'. (Drucker, 1990).

In the NPO there are different objectives and strategies. One key strategic challenge is related to customers. Some managers are reluctant to recognise this, but the *raison d'etre* of most NPOs is about recognising and meeting customers' needs, within tight financial constraints, where the focus is increasingly on value for money and where tighter public spending control is squeezing costs, year after year. NPOs exist only for their customers. It may not always be obvious who the customer is. In many organisations, government is thought to be the customer, but is only a surrogate for the taxpayer. It may also be thought that it is not possible for NPOs to reinvent themselves in the way that some corporations have.

Strategy is also about balancing opportunities and risks. Here the FD has an important role to play. Risks have financial consequences. Every capital appraisal and business plan in the public sector is expected to have both an options appraisal and a risk analysis. Where there is no bottom line to 'sandbag' you, risk is critical. Risk management is of course fundamental to all organisations but in NPOs it needs to be present from planning through to operations.

Corporate planning

From a planning point of view the need, but also the hardest thing, is to get all interested parties to focus on the long term, but this is where agreement is necessary. Once the long term is agreed, short term actions can be compared against the mission and the long term objectives. If short term factors are allowed to prevail, one interest group may prevail over another. Typical strategic corporate plans in the public sector are for a three year period, with a one year business plan (the budget is also fitted to the public spending year, from 1 April to 31 March). This pattern allows for rolling capital spending plans, but still leads to unbalanced spending behaviours because of the threat of losing funds unspent by the financial year end. This occurs not only at department, agency or organisational level, but also within organisations at budget holder level.

In most public sector organisations, the first priority is to balance the books and live within the funds allocated. Increasingly, however, organisations such as the Next Steps Agencies are being encouraged to generate income as well, both to reduce the net cost to government and to fund growing service provision. This prime duty of the FD, of living within means, would be exemplified in, for example, the treasurer (or CFO) of a local authority. A health authority is looking toward the long term health of the nation. The balance should be struck between the long term and short term priorities, through sharing and agreement on the strategic plan. This strikes a balance between the needs of customers, the demands of the surrogate purchaser, the viability of the organisation and the constraint of taxpayers' funds.

Accounting for funds and service gains

The corporate planning culture has led to the widespread adoption of key targets as a means of focusing, motivating and measuring performance in the public sector. The Government White Paper *Better Accounting for the Taxpayer's Money, Resource Accounting and Budgeting in Government* proposed the setting of key objectives and the matching of outputs with inputs for all departments. It has met with practical difficulties, but culture change is under way. Two of the problems are that the financial information systems were designed in a different, cash accounting era, and that there are still relatively few FDs in the public sector with the relevant experience and know-how to implement this bold way forward.

The original aim of implementing resource and accruals accounting within five years, across government, always looked ambitious. The Next Steps Agencies, with their semi-privatised management and greater autonomy, together with the opportunity to build or rebuild systems to cope, may have the best chance. While the Benefits Agency, Contributions Agency and Inland Revenue continue to sit apart, with computer systems which do not talk to each other, however, implementation for a massive proportion of public spending will remain a dream and inefficiency will continue.

The public sector has no profit motive. The prime focus therefore seems to be around the four Es – evaluation, economy, efficiency and effectiveness. The measures of performance should be based on the two Qs: quality, as well as quantity. Of course, measurement of financial performance in the public sector is fundamental, but as the population ages, pensions and benefits bills grow and the government needs to look to a falling number of taxpayers to balance the books, the public will increasingly look for value for money (VFM). In the meantime, resource and accruals accounting could become a red herring or even a white elephant.

Resource accounting goes right to the heart of VFM, efficiency and effectiveness of spending and any self-respecting qualified accountant knows by heart the justification for accruals accounting in showing the real picture. The trouble is that, even if the systems problems could be solved, the complexities of public sector finance, the inconsistency of recommended and applied accounting practices, the artificiality built into the processes by the constraints of the 'public year' and the fact that many major budgets, such as pensions, are funded on a cash basis, are just some of the reasons why the potential real benefits of moving into such a modern world may remain obfuscated. Add to that the burgeoning complexity of accounting standards which are required to be understood and implemented by all CCAB qualified accountants and you see the difficulty.

Measuring performance

The key in a NPO is value for money, whether the money comes from government, the National Lottery, public donations, or whatever. Organisations are now showing not only what the money is spent on, but also how efficiently it is spent. Both tighter budgets and public scrutiny will ensure that a key measure will be the proportion of overhead, administration cost, non-productive expenditure, being minimised. NPOs are tackling this in three main ways: accounting and measuring performance in a way which demonstrates organisational and spending efficiency and effectiveness; cutting costs (although sadly often front-line services are cut as well as support costs); the most creative and responsive are looking at the whole basis of their operations and deciding what they need to do themselves to achieve their agreed service and performance targets, and what they can stop doing or farm out to other, more efficient bodies.

The increasing difficulty, as funds become relatively scarcer, is to balance all the conflicting demands. The role of the FD is to help facilitate optimum efficiency as well as arbitration. Increasingly the tools will be performance measurement and benchmarking with the provision of timely, accurate and usable information. Quality of systems as well as quality of people will be paramount. Quality of spending will be as important as quantity. As well as facilitating the processes of market testing and outsourcing (which may even include the finance department or large parts of it), the FD should lead the process of accountability. It is no longer desirable or acceptable for financial or management information to be centralised, except for the purpose of overall management and review. Delegated responsibility for service should be paralleled by accountability, supported by rapid or even real time information about financial and business consequences, on the service manager's PC.

While financial goals are imposed, increasingly the key discretionary goals are service measures and quality standards. In an era of Citizens' Charters and the new public accountability, many of these goals are highly desirable, if not mandatory. The FD is not immune from this regime – indeed, should set an example. Many people still feel it is impractical or unreasonable to introduce what they see as unachievable private sector, customer oriented practices into the public sector, but meanwhile, several organisations are blazing a trail which a surprising number of private sector companies have not matched.

The London Borough of Brent has been one of these. Unlike some of its local and country cousins, it has not only completed a top to bottom review of its traditional, hierarchical, bureaucratic processes, but has dramatically changed the entire basis of management, finance and service delivery. Working from a core set of values – quality, efficiency, customer focus and empowerment of staff – it has dramatically reduced central overhead, delegated responsibility and accountability to service oriented business units and saved £20m in the process. (*Management Accountant*, December 1996).

There is no reason why a 'balanced scorecard' approach cannot be introduced into a NPO. While for public sector organisations there is the requirement to set and meet targets to satisfy their paymasters, the number of 'key' goals does not need to proliferate – otherwise, some of them cannot be key. Furthermore, in order to motivate people to achieve what will be seen as increasingly challenging goals, it is important not to lose focus. For this reason, there should be a mix of qualitative, as well as quantitative, goals. The FD can take the lead on this and many other aspects.

There is no reason why the finance department should not introduce a quality and customer service programme (after all, everyone is its customer), its own corporate and business plan (integrated with the core plans) and a fundamental review of services, based around economy, efficiency and effectiveness. Having reviewed all its processes and systems, it may well find that the functions to support wider service delivery and devolved accountability can be achieved more economically, e.g. by stopping or outsourcing certain tasks, efficiently (in terms of speed of delivery, so that management information becomes meaningful) and effectively (setting and achieving high customer service and quality standards).

Having implemented similar processes in the NHS Trust we produced a departmental strategic plan; new, Oracle based systems were introduced with distributed financial information; a fundamental review of services was undertaken (and internal audit was outsourced); headcount fell by thirty per cent; and the department budget was cut by twenty per cent in real terms. The same approach across the Trust turned a forecast deficit of £2m to a £3m surplus in six months, tapering down to a balanced budget within three years. The funds released were available for increased patient care and better service provision.

Better service, less administration

The importance of good systems and processes cannot be underestimated. Salaries and wages typically represent a very high proportion of costs in the public sector. As demands for services increase, maximum productivity will be needed to meet challenging performance targets. The last thing service deliverers, such as doctors and nurses, need is to be burdened with excessive or time-consuming administrative procedures. The systems should take the weight and the information provided should be timely and reliable.

A high proportion of costs is for administrators themselves. There should be no need for armies of accountants with clipboards if the targets are clear and shared, the systems and processes are efficient and the information meets the need. The purpose of the FD should be to ensure the availability of information and provide advice, guidance and support where needed. Cost-heavy, labour intensive accounting procedures are an anachronism. Quality is preferable to quantity.

FDs will also play a key role in facilitating change and restructuring. The pattern of services and the way they are delivered is constantly changing. New public service organisations should be built around quality, efficiency and need. Whilst large centralised units may remain for specialist or complex procedures in the NHS for example, scale is breaking down for more general purposes. This parallels changes in industry. The growing pattern will be of slimmed down administration units managing distributed operational units where the need is. These will be more customer friendly and cost-effective. Such changing patterns will place great demands on the FD to help the organisation meet its new challenges while rationalising its outdated stock of assets and its anachronistic organisation.

Old organisations were built around hierarchy and centralised control. No-one had more power than the FD who controlled the purse. New organisations will be built around quality, information and communication, with speed and efficiency of decision and action most important, together with shared understanding of what is to be achieved, why and how and the consequences in performance and financial terms. Review of these will be part of the cycle of continuous improvement which will facilitate greater quality. The forward thinking, open-minded, team playing FD can play a key role in this.

Accountability

This brings me back to accountability. In the modern NPO, accountability is for contribution and results across a range of measures, but most of all for quality. Goals and targets need to be mutually agreed and understood by the whole team. Empowerment of individuals within the team will help optimise performance but understanding of what is to be achieved, how and the availability of relevant timely information are key.

Decisions in a NPO need to be shared and understood. Very few are financial decisions. Each is a management decision with financial consequences. Within a week of arriving in the health service, I was told that a business plan was written from a budget. As FD I set out to change this understanding. A business plan is a series of decisions and planned activities. Each has attendant risks, risks have financial consequences. Each action has a cost, the sum total of these planned costs is a budget. A budget is the quantification of the costs of actions arising from management decisions.

Such a creed is more powerful coming from the FD. It is not an abdication of the FD's role. The FD's role is to lead the process of facilitating the collection and processing of financial information so that the organisation can understand the consequences. Any variance is a variance in achievement against the original plan. That gap requires consequential management action. That action has a cost and financial consequences. These may lead to adjustments to the plan. This does not make the role of the FD passive. He or she is an active member of the team, planning and delivering. The FD's role is no longer to control management action through rationing of finance.

In these respects the FD's role should be no different from the private sector. For as long as performance is quantified in financial terms and money is a scarce resource, the FD's role will be key, but should now be seen as facilitating, not directing, management decisions. If an organisation runs successfully and efficiently, then barring the unforeseen, the only time it should be directed by a finance professional is in receivership or threat of failure – and then only for the short term because the organisation will either be stabilised to allow non-crisis management to be re-established, or to enable sale to or takeover by new management, or it will be wound up. In the public sector, the latter does not happen, but financially based decisions undoubtedly predominate until the organisation is stabilised, usually after a change in management (often including a change in financial management).

Relevance to different organisations

While I have used examples from my own experience in the NHS, consulting with and auditing national and local government, the principles should work for all NPOs. Gone are the days even in voluntary organisations where the FD (or, more likely, accountant) was expected merely to compile the figures. Such organisations cannot sustain themselves without a VFM and, increasingly, commercial approach. Oxfam is now a major retailer. More retired and redundant managers have volunteered for voluntary service to bring commercial ideas and discipline to the most pressing and least visible service delivery.

As with the health service, the education service has seen the arrival of accountability. Published league tables make schools accountable to parents, whose choice of school will be affected by performance success together with intangibles such as standards and values. In addition, accountability is being effected through the medium of funding. As schools are given per capita finance, their educational success or failure will have a direct effect on their potential viability through the consequent level of funding achieved. This cannot be the only factor, otherwise some schools would be empty and others too big to manage. Access and availability are also important.

Schools do not have FDs but they do now need numerate officers, especially the headteacher who is now a manager as much as a vocational leader. The school's board does need high quality financial advice and must always endeavour to include a finance professional among its governors. Retirement and redundancy will produce a growing supply to meet the growing demand. As some schools fail or underperform, increasingly the government is turning to private sector support and methods.

In a NPO there is no bottom line. While there is a temptation to justify existence for altruistic reasons, all NPOs are funded by other agencies, whether they be donors or sponsors in the case of charities, the taxpayers or donors in the case of health, education and local government.

General

> The ultimate question, which I think people in the non-profit organisation should ask again and again and again, both of themselves and the institution is: 'what should I hold myself accountable for by way of contribution and results? What should this institution hold itself accountable for by way of contribution and results?' (Drucker, 1990).

Relationships are even more important in NPOs than companies. There are very many relationships: board, management, people, customers (patients, ratepayers, etc.), donors, sponsors, beneficiaries, national, local and quasi government agencies, professional advisers, professional organisations, unions, interest groups, lobby groups, the community, etc. Whilst not all the needs or requests can be met, all the views need to be taken into account.

Being the FD in a NPO requires diplomatic, political and interpersonal skills no less than the chief executive. The FD has too often in the past been seen as controller of the purse strings. This is no longer appropriate but the FD will always be seen as having power in relation to the money – the lifeblood – of the organisation.

The skill for FDs is to remember that they are first and foremost general managers, possessing the best mix of financial skills and experience and management capability beside the CEO.

The FD cannot afford to sit in an ivory tower, hand down tablets of stone and keep the score. (It is said that in the game of life, accountants were not allowed to play, but were asked to score instead. To get their own back, they made the scoring so complex that nobody could tell who was winning.) The modern FD in any sector participates in all the key management processes to facilitate understanding. Also the FD should build bridges alongside the CEO with all the key principals, agencies and constituencies with which the organisation comes into contact.

FDs should go out of their way to make the information more understandable. A good way is to use 'pictures' – graphs, charts, etc. In too many organisations in both the public and private sectors, the 'numbers bit' is shrouded in mystery. Presentation of financial performance is too often seen as an exercise apart from management performance. The relative lack of numeracy of non-financial managers and the mystique and occasional pomposity of some financial managers allow this dichotomy to continue. This is a gap worth bridging.

A simple management model

Particularly in the NPOs, it is the management and operational performance which should hold the attention. A simple model may help to structure the periodical reports:

- What was the (management) plan?
- What was actually achieved?
- What is the gap?
- What are the reasons for the gap?
- What can be done to remedy the situation (or better still, what is already being done)?
- What are the consequences (including financial)?
- What can we learn from this (i.e. how can we improve in future)?

Note that the financial consequences are not the first consideration (not to say they are not important). A budget quantifies the financial value of agreed management decisions and actions. The financial report quantifies what has actually been achieved and gives a financial scale to problems.

Public sector organisations such as hospital trusts and local authorities are often large and widely distributed. In these, no less than elsewhere, it is important that the FD or equivalent is visible and available. The FD should meet key internal customers on a regular basis and thereby maintain a good 'feel' for the organisation's progress and financial wellbeing. As with the private sector, the chief financial manager is the CEO's most important team member but also should be able to rely on their superior's numeracy.

Motivation in NPOs

Quality, efficiency in delivery, altruism, etc. are key motivators where there is no profit. Pay has not been so important in the past – salary levels have been well below the private sector. This does not necessarily mean that quality is worse. I have met and worked with many talented professionals in the public sector who could operate effectively in the private sector, given sufficient time to learn and adjust, especially to the faster pace. The salary gap closed as a result of the recession and skills transfer (although it has widened again as the economy has improved). Working in the public sector provides a different set of challenges for the FD. In addition, there is the personal reward of a contribution to society. Also, the public sector is undergoing continuous change and challenge.

The number of volunteers in NPOs is increasing, partly as they are seen as adding to 'citizenship'. Charities and charitable organisations, schools, and so on are seeing more unpaid volunteers, especially at governance level. Quangos are also taking more people on. The remuneration at board level is low compared to non-executive directorships in the private sector. People accept a different set of challenges for a different kind of motivation. This in no way should belittle the level of contribution. There are differences in how governing bodies are appointed. Some are selected, some appointed and some co-opted.

NPOs are also information based flowing in all directions – top down and bottom up. People management should be based around team and individual performance towards shared and agreed goals, in keeping with the organisation's mission. This is why mission is critical. If money (personal or corporate) does not motivate people, then service to the cause and to people, making a clear contribution to an understood mission, is what satisfies.

Management development is critical, as some finance staff have left to return to a recovering private sector. Counselling and empowerment are powerful tools. Losing someone good to the competition as a result of personal development is not a total disaster. Your organisation has enjoyed and benefited from the partnership with that person. Your reputation benefits from that person becoming a committed ambassador moving elsewhere. Team and individual performance can improve dramatically in an environment of real empowerment. When someone moves on, someone else moves up. In an organisation good at internal development, everyone benefits. As someone said 'when the chief executive retires, we end up promoting a clerk'.

Change and financial challenges for the future

NPOs are among the biggest employers in the UK. The NHS is the biggest single employer in Europe. What is more, even in hard times, the consumption of NPOs in the UK has increased in real terms. There is a funding crisis which faces us in the 21st century (and all developed countries). In a recent OECD report, the UK came out better than some. Whereas it was felt that pensions could be funded throughout the next century without increasing taxation, in Germany it would require 93% of GDP and in Japan 238% of GDP. For anyone there is a formidable challenge when health, welfare and education are added in. Already two workers in the UK support two non-workers (including children and the elderly).

Change is inevitable and the challenges will be great for the FD. There will need to be rationing, different ways of delivering service, greater efficiency, etc. Even now, it does not take much to find inefficiency in the public sector, including a much higher proportion of non-productive, administrative and other support costs than in the private sector. Look at what has happened in the privatised industries. Hundreds of thousands of jobs have been dispensed with, prices have been cut, service standards and quality have been improved and still these companies (e.g. electricity and water companies) have run at profit levels that have provoked a public outcry, where formerly they drained the public purse. BT and others are among the best performing in their industries in the world.

As the public purse becomes tighter and demands for public services grow, society will have to make choices. One of these is whether the public sector has a function to provide underproductive employment to people who would otherwise be unemployed. If so, there will be consequences in higher taxation. It is likely that rationalisation will continue in the public sector. As service demands increase the FD will advise that support functions must become more efficient and cost-effective. Otherwise, FDs and their equivalent will find it harder to balance the books.

Budgeting and spending

Cost cutting as a practice is endemic in the public sector. In the past it has not been unusual for the CEO or the FD to 'red line' budgets to balance the books. Characteristically, organisations look at what they need to do and the funds available, and cut their cloth accordingly. As increasing productivity is needed to balance burgeoning service demands with tight public finance, cost improvement programmes have become the order of the day. My view is that these have become counterproductive.

The modern FD uses a different approach. The business plan is an agreed summary of the agreed activities for the coming year, after all bids, interests, demands, etc. have been taken into account, reviewed and discussed. When the financial consequences of the plan are evaluated (by the functional and departmental managers, facilitated by the finance function) the total projected costs will often exceed the funds available. The matter is further complicated because in an ever changing world, budgets will increasingly need to be flexible and funds will also need to be available to manage unpredictable change. These should be under the sole direction of the CEO, but biddable by any department in a competitive process.

Formerly, the FD or Treasurer controlled the spending process. Contingency funds and 'back pocket accounting' proliferated. A proportion of funds were kept back and played out as needed by the FD. This encouraged bad budgeting.

The modern FD should be able to challenge all budgets, if necessary line by line, but always accompanied by the relevant director. The latter should challenge or defend the need for the basis of the spending (i.e. the underlying activity). The FD should challenge the need to spend and help by advising the CEO on conflicting needs and priorities. The ultimate arbiter is the CEO (or even the board where there are strategic consequences).

Unfortunately, in the public sector, the FD or treasurer may often be held directly accountable if financial targets are not met. While this encourages greater control, a good FD and a good MD in partnership working within the right team environment can lead and facilitate the process to achieve the same ends. This must be better than the old-fashioned FD's red pencil.

> Non profits need management even more than business does, precisely because they lack the discipline of the bottom line. The non profits are, of course, still dedicated to 'doing good.' But they also realise that good intentions are no substitute for organisation and leadership, for accountability, performance and results. These require management and that, in turn, begins with the organisation's mission. (Drucker, 1990).

This is the essential difference.

> Businesses start their planning with the financial returns. Non profits start with the performance of their mission.

This is a lesson businesses can learn. It focuses on action and the strategies needed to achieve the goals. It creates discipline. The focus needs to be on the mission and the results achieved towards, and in the context of, the mission.

> There are at first sight unique differences between the public and private sector. Further examination, however, of what characterises these differences leads me to the view that individually they are not in fact unique but that they mirror the wide range of businesses that can be found outside the public sector. However, there are some factors at the extremes of the range of variables which will influence how we operate. What is unique is finding them all under one umbrella – that of

national government.....Without the clarity that comes from the influence of market forces, a bottom line and return to shareholders, adopting private sector management techniques is more challenging than most people would think. But application of the concepts can certainly achieve the result which we all seek – of giving greater value for money to our customers and the taxpayer. (Sir Michael Partridge, Permanent Secretary, Department of Social Security in *Management Today*, November 1994).

Accounting practices

It is undeniable that despite growing convergence and skills transfer between private and public sector accounting practices (hopefully with each benefiting from best practice in the other), there will remain differences and issues which arise therefrom.

NPOs are different and particularly where they are publicly funded, capital project justification and accounting will be different. This is not to say that return on capital will not be a common measure, but for example the rate of return required in the public sector is usually much lower than the private sector. There is no profit motive and some public schemes need to go forward for reasons beyond bare financial cost-benefit analysis. This brings into consideration non-financial measures which will supplement financial indicators where there is no bottom line.

The form of public statements will differ in the NPO sector, for example disclosing more to a wider audience, including government and the public. Accounting practices and standards may vary, not just in relation to capital valuation and depreciation (where some of the practices are ludicrous) but also the use of cash accounting rather than the accruals basis. Although this is related to the treasury's need to manage the public finances on a discrete year basis, it has led to a number of unacceptable paradoxes including the bunching of expenditure in March (the end of the financial year) which makes it very difficult to control costs, and the mixed adoption of the accruals concept.

The White Paper referred to earlier sought to address this inconsistency, but the differing levels of capability, the differing degrees of autonomy and, most of all, the inadequacy, obsolescence and incoherence of information systems, mean that a pattern of unbalanced progress across government will further complicate public accounting. Until resource and accruals accounting is successfully introduced across government, the desired public accountability, control, efficiency and effectiveness of public spending cannot be optimised.

More than a change in accounting practices will be needed. There are policy changes which stand in the way. Most obviously, what is the point of introducing accruals accounting, when two of the biggest budgets are unfunded? (Benefits and pensions are still funded on a cash basis). Government raises taxes (through income tax and NI contributions) on one side of the account, and pays out pensions, benefits and the costs of healthcare on the other side. The Inland Revenue and Contributions Agency systems are not integrated; the Contributions Agency and the Benefits Agency have closer links, being part of the DSS, but again the systems are not integrated. Pensions and war pensions are in other agencies. Pensions and Social Security are the two biggest financial headaches for government in the 21st century, but although steps have been taken to move towards private sector management for new pensions, for as long as any adult alive today reaches and remains at pensionable age, cash accounting will be mixed with accruals accounting.

Presenting financial information

The way financial information is presented to external and internal audiences is very much a function of the nature of the public sector organisation and even more than in the private sector, it is desirable that it should be congruent between the two. There is little worse than presenting two sets of information and then trying to explain or reconcile the differences. If the information comes from a common source, it should appear to show the same meaning. In any sector, apparent differences lead to unnecessary confusion or even suspicion. The ideal for the FD is to prepare the information in a form which is suitable for everyone. For example, the board of a NHS trust should see the same picture that is presented to their regional managers for regulatory reasons.

Preparing financial information in one form for public consumption and in another, labour-intensive way for one's paymasters and regulatory purposes only adds to inefficiency and confusion. As a result, when I joined the public sector, the monthly information for regulatory purposes was required within 20 business days of the month end (i.e. one month). This distorted the reporting timetable for management and resulted in two separate sets of financial information being produced. It was impossible to reconcile the two adequately. Within 12 months, we had brought down our own deadline to eight business days, but the information was still virtually meaningless to service managers running a quality and efficiency oriented, sharp-end service function.

With budget implementation and distribution being completed up to three months after the start of the financial year (or worse, in some cases), this illustrates the difficulty of managing in the public sector with inadequate or unfocused information. Things have improved, but still public services drown in a sea of paper and information systems remain unintegrated. All this costs money.

There are many other issues. One way forward is for regular dialogue between financial officers from different organisations and also by using professional auditors to help ensure best practice, consistency and commonality.

There are no FDs in many parts of the public sector, e.g. the treasury or the civil service. Whether there are or not, the person performing the closest approximation to the role is recommended to be aware of and adopt best practice, including, where appropriate, best commercial practice. Transparency will increasingly be demanded in NPOs and commonality of accounting practice, especially applying high standards, will help to build trust. In all such organisations, the role of the FD or equivalent remains to lead and facilitate the production of the financial information and collate it with non-financial measures of performance to enable the organisation to judge its progress towards agreed goals and against agreed plans. Over and above that the FD or chief financial officer should be available to provide advice, guidance and support, not only on the information but on financial and funding planning, strategy, policy and management. This is no different from the standards to be expected in private sector organisations, nor is the requirement to lead the setting and implementation of the highest standards of governance, as described in Chapter 8.

While the relevant skills may not always be available to NPOs, the transfer of those skills from the private sector will increase through design and circumstance. I will leave the final word to David Timson of N B Selection:

> Experience of cultural diversity will therefore, I believe, be one of the critical requirements for new financial directors of international businesses. Whereas in the past it was tempting to look either internally for people who 'really know our business' or externally from those from a similar industry sector, our clients are now often looking for 'hands on' experience of living and working in different parts of the world. Very often, they also prefer finance directors from a very different industry sector who will bring new ideas and a different perspective to the board, hopefully adding competitive advantage. (Timson, 1995).

Taken with Yvonne Sarch's comments earlier and other experience in the public sector, we can see a changing picture where flexibility, adaptability, vision and leadership will become more valuable than steadfast experience in one industry or even with one employer. In a global marketplace, insularity will be a disadvantage.

The Private Finance Initiative (PFI)

I do not propose to write a treatise here on the PFI. However, it is here to stay, as is the process of quasi-privatisation of government. The reasons are clear. Primarily the public purse cannot continue to afford the burgeoning benefits, healthcare and pensions needs of an aging population; also, the private sector has many skills, especially in the matter of understanding and meeting customers' service needs, that the public sector either does not have, or cannot afford. I shall restrict my comment to the relevance of the PFI to FDs in both the private and public sectors.

The PFI got off to a disappointing start, for four main reasons.

- Introduced by a Conservative government, it was always going to be an easy target for Labour, who attacked it as 'privatisation by stealth'.

- The approval procedures and the required financial targets for a scheme to be approved (including passing the majority of the risk to the private sector) were difficult or impossible to achieve (and often took two or three years to complete).

- Ignorance of how each other worked and different expectations between the private and public sectors (most notably the profit motive), together with little or no background or experience in the public sector to judge, evaluate, manage or implement mould-breaking schemes (augmented by politically motivated resistance in some quarters, especially as a likely change of government approached).

- Different structures in the two sectors, especially the inability of most of the public sector to create sole or joint venture limited companies.

This was particularly frustrating for many FDs coming from the private sector. Their motivation was to save money while improving service quality and efficiency, their training and practical backgrounds had not been restricted by the major obstacles to progress in the public sector. Furthermore, while the private sector worked with and understood corporate finance and the city, the public sector had been excluded from such experience. The result – frustration all round, especially in government, where the desired financial efficiencies and the progress of major projects fell well below the optimistic projections.

FDs in both sectors are at the heart of PFI projects. The new government has quietly adopted the PFI as policy, and private sector involvement and management in sectors previously as sacrosanct as education is moving forward steadily. The PFI represents both a challenge and an opportunity for FDs. The challenge to understand new methods, structures, financing arrangements and the evaluation of complex capital and management projects; the opportunity to facilitate major service improvement, deliver greater financial efficiency and unlock funding for pressing service needs (as well as relying less on the public purse).

The purpose of the PFI was to bring commercial experience and nous, innovation and management to public sector projects, as well as private sector funds to ease the public sector burden – especially in the case of aging infrastructure. The privatisation of gas, water and electricity was already proving a success in this respect – could PFI do the same for hospitals, schools, roads, bridges and tunnels, housing, public buildings? The Next Steps Agencies were beginning to show what greater autonomy could do for management efficiency, again by importing e.g. private sector FDs, could PFI do the same for management of public services? The progress of outsourcing of support services was giving a good steer.

Since the election, some positive signs have emerged. The new government has not only loosened red tape and speeded up procedures, it has also created a Treasury PFI Taskforce, with its own chief executive, and several schemes have been approved. A move to standard documentation, centralisation of the approval procedures, the learning curve for negotiations and relief that the PFI will not be abolished has breathed new energy into the initiative. There is still a degree of ignorance, inertia and political opposition in some sectors. In addition, local authorities still need clarification on whether restrictions on reuse of released housing capital will be eased and whether PFI schemes will be caught by capping. Furthermore, much of the public is still sceptical about hospitals and schools being 'privatised'.

In the meantime, if the current progress is maintained, there is much to go for for both the private and public sectors. The impact on FDs in both sectors could be widespread. In the public sector, it will further increase financial complexity and workloads, especially in the area of capital spending. On the other hand, it could help create a climate whereby additional sources of income and the business and legal structures to generate them could be loosened up – especially the ability to set up limited companies. This latter power is already available to the education sector, where universities have entered into joint ventures and established companies to manage student accommodation and even run hotels and conference facilities.

For the private sector, there are opportunities for a diverse range of contractors – from those who build major capital projects, to capital equipment suppliers, IT and IS suppliers and other service suppliers and contractors. In order to maximise the opportunity for both sectors, FDs should understand the normal practices of the party on the other side of the table, together with the City of London, its capital markets and corporate finance processes. Otherwise, projects will remain stalled or miss the boat, or worse still, the financial consequences could be steep. Having worked in all three roles, I can see continuing opportunities for consultants to facilitate and inform projects and some potential for continuing frustration, waste of time and money. In four or five years time, it will have been abolished, or it will have led the way forward to a new mixed economy of public/private sector funding in public sectors.

4

The FD as director and strategist

Although sometimes referred to as the CFO, the FD should always have a board role. One of the main reasons is the strong trend towards FDs leading the strategic processes of the organisation. The FD has traditionally been expected to have feet firmly on the ground. The FD is also expected to be a strategist, even if only in the context of financial strategy. The pace of change of the modern world is manageable in the short term, unpredictable in the long term and appears to conform to natural models in the very long term. The (usually) rational FD is expected to lead the formulation of strategy in an economic world experiencing increasing volatility and also now subject to global pressures.

One of the primary functions of the board of directors is to agree the organisation's long term strategy. Ideally the chief executive leads this process, but the plan should be proposed by management. Increasingly the FD is being asked to take the lead. If anything demonstrates the breadth of challenge now facing FDs, it is the spectrum which goes from leading a process which is trying to plot the organisation's course through long range uncertainty, while at the same time being expected to report the consequences of previous plans and keep an eye on viability and probity. The FD is not only first and foremost a director, but is also usually charged with leading stewardship and governance. The strategic planning aspects of the role will be developed in Chapter 10 on Planning.

An executive director

> There are few functions on the main board which have such a helicopter view of the entire company and its strengths and weaknesses. I would say without a strong finance function and finance director, with the pace of change all companies must face today, the likelihood of consistent success in the future for that corporation is remote. (Keith Oates, 1995, Deputy Chairman, Marks & Spencer).

David Timson also wrote about change:

> One of our multinational clients.....has now completely dismantled its divisional structure, and all its businesses report directly to the chief executive. There are now only three executive directors on the main board – the chief executive, the finance director and a corporate affairs director who is responsible for all other functions, including human resources, corporate communication, company secretarial work and so on. This sort of change is quite typical of what is likely to

> happen in the future. The Cadbury Committee emphasis on the importance of non-executive directors also tends to encourage it. Given the practical number of people who can effectively sit round a table and get anything done is limited to about ten, if there are to be more non-executive directors, there will inevitably be fewer executive directors. (Timson, 1995).

This will be a dramatic change for some companies which in the past have operated solely with executives – and a welcome one too. Cadbury, Hampel and others have looked into the role of the board. The prime aspects should be: to select a chairman and appoint a chief executive (the other directors, while appointed by the board and approved by the shareholders or their equivalent, would be recommended by the chairman, in the case of NEDs, and the CEO, in the case of executive directors); to approve the recommended strategic plan and its associated consequences; to protect the shareholders' interests; and to set a clear purpose and policies for operation. There remain three areas for further progress: more, suitable NEDs; the centrality of a shared vision, purpose and goals as a focus for the board; and the dearth of treasury skills.

While the balance of NED and executive director may be changing, it is still recommended that the most senior financial manager in an organisation should ideally have a place on the board (see also the Cadbury report recommendation.) The Barings case also highlighted the desperate need for there to be at least one non-executive, as well as an FD or treasury director, who understands treasury and risk management. This theme recurs later in the book, but it is a major failing that companies have still not moved forward with this aspect. Lack of suitable candidates is no excuse, with over 2000 members of the Institute of Corporate Treasurers, many working as consultants or executive directors of other companies.

Any references to the FD would also include the holder of the equivalent role. The legal situation described later in this chapter tends to accept that whatever the title, a director performing the role cannot escape the liability when things go wrong. This is as good a reason as any to always formalise the role. As the reader should be clear by now, it is one of great responsibility, second only to the Chief Executive in the management team and therefore one which will demand the very best skills and a broader, more adaptable incumbent than before.

Responsibility and governance

Being a director of a company is a serious matter. Stephen Tromans and Gillian Irvine make it clear that 'where a company is guilty of an offence, a director or similar officer of the company may also be guilty in certain circumstances'. (Tromans and Irvine, 1994).

Also, the law now provides for disqualification of directors in certain circumstances where a company has failed, or the director has been guilty of fraud. Even where a finance director has been directed by the chairman or managing director to perform or support unlawful acts, the FD would not escape responsibility. The 1986 Company Directors' Disqualification Act was designed to protect companies from dishonest or serially incompetent directors. While 1996 saw a seventy per cent rise in disqualifications, a report published by CCN in 1997 showed more than 4000 directors who had been involved in more than ten company failures.

It is not unusual for the FD to be in a position of conflicting loyalties. As much as any other director, the FD should be trained for and must be aware of the corporate governance responsibility of a director. Furthermore, the FD is equipped to calculate or estimate the known or likely financial consequences of a particular course of action.

The most difficult situation facing a FD is where there is a potential conflict between responsibility to the MD (or collective cabinet responsibility) and responsibility as a director. In all cases, the latter must override the former. If there is a valid concern, especially where dishonesty or deceit is involved, the first and proper course is to draw the attention of the MD to the problem. In the event that the MD is unwilling to act, the next recourse is to the chairman of the board. Where the MD is guilty of a fraudulent or illegal act, the first recourse must be to the chairman.

There is no escaping this governance responsibility, especially for the FD. While FDs may sometimes find themselves in a position of disagreeing with a particular policy or strategy and should exercise their judgement as to the optimum course of action, where an illegal act is contemplated or has been committed, there is only one course of action.

Increasingly, these days, the FD has responsibility for the audit function. Problems may often arise through discovery in the audit process. Inability to apply the right judgement invalidates any justification for the FD to carry this responsibility. The value of the audit committee should not be underestimated in this situation, as it confers access to the board for the internal or external auditor when things go wrong.

A finance director must be mindful that he or she is both a manager and a director. Assumed to have the most appropriate skills to consider financial consequences, the position of FD is in some ways the most difficult director's role of all. Not surprisingly, when things go wrong, FDs are sometimes asked to look for new employment.

The Cadbury report on *The Financial Aspects of Corporate Governance* recommends that:

> boards should recognise the importance of the finance function by making it the designated responsibility of a main board director.

The report recognised that:

> in law, all directors are responsible for the stewardship of the company's assets. All directors, therefore, whether or not they have executive responsibilities, have a monitoring role and are responsible for ensuring that the necessary controls.....are in place and working.

If this is true for all directors, it is particularly so for finance directors. It would be reasonable for the board or its audit committee to expect to seek the advice of the FD on matters relating to finance and control. There is no toss of a coin where conflict arises. The board interest overrides the management interest. The board is appointed to protect the shareholders/stakeholders interests. If it fails, it should expect appropriate consequences. This might lead to the departure of the FD, or even MD.

In the public sector, things are not very different. In NHS trusts, for example, there has been a strict regime of financial performance. (In addition, trusts are expected to show growing value for money.) In the event of consistent underachievement on these targets, or a loss of confidence in the likelihood of achieving them under the existing management, the chairman, chief executive and finance director could be held accountable and their positions would be at risk. It would not be unusual for the FD to be an early casualty.

The legal position of the FD as a director

Much of this section has been put together with reference to the Companies Act 1985 and an excellent book by Loose and Yelland, *The Company Director*, 1987.

The FD is first and foremost a director. The elements of the role as a director are, in law: agent; trustee; master and servant; and independent contractor.

As an agent, the FD is deemed to be acting on behalf of the company. If this is within authority, the company is liable. If outside the authority, the FD may be liable to a third party for breach of the warranty of authority. The FD must account to the company (principal) for any personal profit made out of the position as FD.

As trustee, any assets in the FD's hands are held on behalf of the company. The fiduciary duty of the FD is to ensure that personal interests do not conflict with duties to the company. This position is clear in law, but I am always surprised at the lack of judgement of some people. As a servant of the company, one knows instinctively that the company comes first. It is better not to embark on any venture which may involve a director deriving some benefit for themselves, then there is no possibility of conflict. So why do people arrange contracts with outside organisations which they control or have a declarable interest in and overlook the wisdom of this or even the need to declare it? Too often it leads to problems. If such a contract were to put the individual's financial status at risk, or if it led to a dispute, the temptation is to let the personal interest override the company's interest. The honourable step is to resign. Better yet to avoid such a contract in the first place.

Although executive directors are salaried employees (servants), they wear the master's hat as well. As independent contractor 'there seems no reason why a chartered accountant appointed as FD should not be expected to show the same objective standard of skill and care as if he were engaged in the work as a private practitioner.' (Loose and Yelland, 1987).

The director is also an officer for the purposes of the Act, e.g. where the company or an officer is in default. The question then is – who are directors? The answers are:

- a person duly appointed in relation to the Articles and not since disqualified is a director for all purposes;

- a person appointed with some defect in his appointment; so far as third parties are concerned his acts are validated by s.285 of the Act;

- a person never appointed at all but nevertheless performing the functions of a director (hence my view that it is equitable to formalise the position, otherwise they can incur all the responsibilities and penalties but without the authority of a proper appointment.)

In general, anyone can be a director unless disqualified for some reason. The Articles define the powers of the directors. The duties are partly couched in the elements of the role. In addition, the director has a duty to the company and thereby its shareholders and also a duty to act in good faith where there is a genuine belief that such acts are in the company's interests. As a trustee the director is expected to apply skill and care.

All directors are expected to have an understanding of the company's affairs and its business but in respect of the finances, the FD is expected to understand more and apply appropriate skills and care to the role. Nevertheless, all directors are collectively responsible for the company's acts.

Every company must prepare a financial report and accounts. There are several information requirements for the report. Accounts are expected to show a true and fair view (although the Accounting Standards Board has often wrestled with what this means). The model of report for companies has now been widely applied in other sectors in various forms, e.g. building societies and NHS Trusts. The most notable departure is that these latter organisations have disclosed much more, together with meeting their own regulatory requirements.

I referred earlier to the problem of disquiet or dissent in a practical example. Where a director is concerned about the legality of acts or the standards of conduct of the company, there are a number of possible courses of action:

- vote against the proposal and record the reasons for dissent;

- seek legal advice from the company's lawyers;

- express the view in the company's general meeting;

- resign (after carefully considering this action) but the shareholders should be told the reasons for resigning and the company should come first. Resignation is better for the individual than removal but the director still has the right to make a statement;

- where a director considers that the actions of colleagues involve serious irregularities, the DTI may be approached to intervene and appoint inspectors under the act;

- sometimes as a member of the company a director can seek the assistance of the courts against fellow directors, although under Foss v. Harbottle, the court will not generally interfere in internal affairs;

- in an extreme case a director may feel that the only solution is to put the company into liquidation.

Now all of the above may seem quite drastic and it must be stressed that any director, especially the FD must explore all other possible avenues first. These start with the chief executive, the chairman and the board, unless they are criminally implicated. Fortunately, most of the instances of dissent occur in private companies. I will leave it to the reader to speculate on the effect on the company's share price and viability if such action were taken by the director of a plc. When Ferranti discovered major fraud in the contracts of a company it had acquired, it rapidly led to Ferranti having to be taken over by a competitor.

Finally, a director, especially the FD, can be expected to act in a professional manner. The Institute of Directors is the relevant and highly regarded professional body. The FD as a professional is dealt with in Chapter 17.

Strategic planning and direction

Whether by design or default, this role has increasingly been assigned to the FD. This was true in both the private and public sector organisations where I was FD.

It is not surprising that the two roles are often combined, except that not all accountants are creative or visionaries. A strategic business plan usually includes a substantial amount of quantification. Sadly, however, some so-called business plans appear to have little else. Even a one year plan needs a strategic context. This would usually be a long-term vision, mission or goals and a 3/5 year strategic framework.

A strategic plan must be a team effort. While it may often be prepared by management, where the production does not involve the board it must be approved by the board. The board should be the strategic and policy forum for any organisation.

The surveys mentioned earlier indicated how rapidly strategic planning is assuming importance as a role for the FD. The FD may lead the process, but it would be ideally facilitated by someone with the appropriate skills and experience. Where these do not exist in the organisation, an appropriately skilled management consultant may be called on. This approach has the added benefit that the consultant is an impartial outsider.

While the strategic planning team does not need to be composed entirely of top management and directors, it does need to be able to draw on a range of experience and interest covering all the key functions of the enterprise. Strategic or creative thinking capability are not possessed by all managers. It has been useful in some circumstances to set up two teams: the top team to lead the strategic process; and a shadow team at deputy level which carries out much of the heavy work and number crunching that goes into working up the plan from the original session.

The FD should be able to draw on his or her own general management capability to ensure that the resulting plan is rounded, takes account of all appropriate needs and interests, covers both the long and shorter terms, macro and micro, the enterprise, its environment and marketplace. Not many accountants possess the necessary skills without broader experience and development. By the time they reach the FD level, they should be regarded as general managers as well as financial managers. Part of the skill set of a good MD or FD is to be able to ask the right questions, in respect of any key function or operation in the organisation.

Strategic leadership

Ideally the MD would lead the strategic planning process, but in the event that this has been delegated to the FD, the MD should be able to rely on a broad understanding of the organisation, impartiality and objectivity, as well as taking for granted the financial skills to quantify the consequences and risks of failure.

> Strategic planning has become both more simple and more complicated in the last ten years. Simple because no-one seems any longer to believe in the cumbersome, model driven central planning department. More complicated because in the absence of that resource you nonetheless have to ensure that the strategic planning process addresses the key issues and comes up with robust responses. The art is therefore of ensuring that there is adequate involvement in the strategic planning process for people to take ownership while at the same time ensuring flexibility as external circumstances might change. Of course this is not necessarily the role of the FD if the chief executive is of a strategic bent. Funnily though, FDs always seem to be involved. (R N Chisman, 1995, Financial Director, Stakis plc).

Chapter 10 deals with the FD's role as planning manager, but strategy, financial direction, stewardship and governance are the foremost responsibilities of the FD. It is important to set what comes later in a strategic context.

> You must have long range goals to keep you from being frustrated by short-term failures. (Charles C Noble).

> A lot in life and business is totally unpredictable. Of course you have to plan ahead, research your markets, make sure you've got the right people and resources and strategy for new business ventures. But there are some things you can forecast and other things you can't and sometimes you have to go ahead because you believe instinctively that an action or investment is the right thing. We surround ourselves with forecasts and computer models for comfort, but everybody knows these are all speculative; and you can waste hours debating sets of financial projections, none of which have any bearing on future reality. (Alan Wilson, 1996, Chief Executive, Anglian Water).

The answer is probably somewhere between these two positions. The question is how does an organisation set strategy in a rapidly changing ('Chaotic'), volatile environment, beset by global factors and competition? In Peter Drucker's book *Managing for the Future* (1992), he makes it clear that exporting is not sufficient. You need market based manufacture in order to get market share (a good reason for British companies to set up manufacturing facilities in China). The key economic driver is investment. The FD wants to see a return on that investment, net of currency fluctuations. The matter of whether these are set too high in the UK is discussed elsewhere, but maybe this is no surprise when so much risk exists. Equally this explains the shorter payback periods now required. Technology has only given us a momentary edge in what Tom Peters called the 'nanosecond nineties'. How should an FD act as a strategist in such an environment?

In *The New Manager's Handbook* (1990, edited by Michael Armstrong), Ralph Stacey described dynamic strategic management as:

> that political form of learning which we practise when we do not know what we are doing; it is also the continuous balancing of two diametrically opposed forms of control. Dynamic strategic management cannot, therefore, be installed in advance of change as a set of plans, structures or systems. Nor can it be some prearranged vision and shared values. It can only be encouraged to occur by the politically powerful in a business when they establish the conditions favourable to a functional political activity and complex group learning. While we can say something in general about what those favourable conditions might be, there are no tried and tested models available for simple installation. Each organisation must discover and develop for itself those conditions which will enable it to manage strategically and dynamically.

He develops these thoughts further in *Dynamic Management for the 1990s* and *Dynamic Management and Scientific Chaos*. (Stacey, 1994).

Managing change

So how is the FD to lead strategy in a changing world? Stacey defines two styles of strategic management – rational planning and entrepreneurial enthusiasm. Whatever the FD decides, colleagues must support wholeheartedly, especially where they are at the sharp end of operational responsibility.

In my opinion and experience, all organisations can benefit from a mission – an undated purpose to strive for (as long as it is specific, definable, meaningful and lasting).

Organisations are at last appreciating the value of visionary leadership to guide, direct and motivate people with different personal values, choices and drivers to 'sign up' for the long term.

A long term plan (probably three years these days) gives an overall structure and direction for those activities which remain the same and those which arise from the more or less predictable consequences of change in the organisation and its environment. The plan needs to be dynamic, however, not just the result of an annual ritual which is filed and not looked at until next year.

Critical to the success of managing for open-ended change is a dynamic organisation with clear but flexible management processes, high standards of quality (constantly under review for improvement), superb relevant information and highly motivated, adaptable, innovative, 'intrapreneurial' people. It goes without saying that the FD should be in the same mould, in order to lead by example.

Manageable and predictable change can be dealt with through the monthly planning review process with actions adapted to respond to change as it occurs.

Unpredictable, or open-ended change needs management processes which allow for the involvement and contribution of all relevant parties, open discussion directed at understanding the problem or opportunity and entrepreneurial management and people empowered to take advantage of opportunities which present themselves and become accepted as new or incremental strategy.

Information management

In such a management environment, there are enormous challenges for the providers of information and those expected to lead the control of resources – not least the FD.

Information systems need to be flexible, adaptable and readily accessible as well as superb. Modelling will proliferate but this should not override the value of intuition and the need for judgement. Systems must also cater for innovation in processes and products. This may become continuous.

So what is the FD's place in all this? As previously implied, the modern FD needs above all to be a facilitator, advisor and guide to ensure that management has the information it needs to make informed judgements and is fully aware of the consequences of its decisions. Among the skills of the FD, bean counting and number crunching have been replaced by forecasting, predicting, modelling, assessing, balancing, judging, supporting, etc.

Flexibility, adaptability and innovation are the key. Financial information systems have moved from inflexible, outdated, centralised accounting systems to adaptable, decentralised, real-time, hands-on systems available to all relevant parties through a shared network, or even the Internet or an intranet. (Some organisations are already giving customers access to their networks as part of the partnership.)

This does not mean the end of accounting. As well as enabling managers to understand the consequences of actions in an environment of accelerating change, the FD will still need to ensure that systems exist to capture and consolidate history, highlight divergence from plan and facilitate the control and management of scarce resources. If the processes and systems can balance these two apparently conflicting needs – historical accounting and facilitation of understanding – it is then up to management to justify its actions in the light of the original plan and the changed environment.

This is not to say that the FD can be absolved from the process of explanation and justification. The FD is an integral part of the team and shares responsibility for agreed actions. At the same time the FD has a responsibility to draw attention to the risks of such actions, especially when these threaten the legality, stability or viability of the organisation. This is the process of governance. It needs to be so impartial that the FD is seen both as wholehearted participant in anticipated change and as steward of the financial viability of the organisation.

People management

Of course this is not just a solitary function, but this is where the people management skills of the FD come into play. As financial planning and financial management stretch across a widening spectrum, selection and development of the right people for the finance function will be critical. As high quality systems and processes are developed, quality of the individual replaces quantity. Checking processes can be eliminated as managers become truly accountable for their own performance and the information which defines it. Except for routine functions such as financial services (debtors, creditors, cash management, payroll, etc.) which are being increasingly outsourced, the size of the finance function will decrease, but the quality will improve. As the rest of the organisation becomes leaner and flatter, finance will be seen as an overhead needing to be justified to its customers (i.e. everyone else in the organisation).

The values, character and style of the finance people need to reflect the overall values, character and style of the organisation. If finance is seen as old-fashioned, one-paced or resistant to change it will become detached from the mainstream of the organisation and may hold back the organisation's natural pace of development or entrepreneurial style. Worse still, its input and information may be rejected, leading to local anarchy, locally developed information systems and a growing problem of integrating and reconciling reported corporate performance. This is not to eschew decentralised operations and support systems which have become more the order of the day, but the FD still has a job to do in collating organisation-wide performance, both historical and predicted. To do so there must be a partnership and a shared sense of purpose with all parts of the organisation.

If the challenges of people management will be great for everyone in the new dynamic organisation, they may be greatest for the FD. In addition to adapting to the new style themselves, or risking being squeezed out, FDs will need to lead the process of change in the finance function. Accountants are not ordinarily intuitive, empowering and dynamic, tending instead to be seen as logical, controlling and less flexible in manner and outlook than some of their colleagues. By far the biggest set of challenges is for the FDs (or equivalent) in SMEs. Their role is as broad as anywhere (often encompassing IT/IS and even personnel functions, as well as the expected core).

It is no accident that more women are coming through in finance functions. Apart from the professions seeing more than 50% female entry at the trainee stage for accountancy, women tend to be more intuitive, creative, team and people oriented. They are also often better listeners. However these characteristics came about, they will increasingly be valued, whereas in the past a more macho, rational, logical, autocratic style of management has prevailed. This change in approach is clear in many parts of the public sector, where the number of women managers and directors in finance functions is growing rapidly.

'Here is my decision – do it!' has given way to a process which anticipates, understands and manages for change with new ideas and opportunity for input welcomed from all relevant parties before moving forward with agreed actions – sometimes resulting in a change in strategic direction.

A key player in every one of these teams will be someone who can not only facilitate the understanding of risks and financial consequences of various courses of action before moving forward, but who will also participate wholeheartedly in both the understanding and management processes. Interpersonal skills and general management capability will be highly valued in the FD. The latter is the subject of the next chapter before returning to the FD's financial responsibilities.

This chapter has been very much about the FD's high level responsibilities as a director and strategist. The pattern of the book has now been set – to examine all the various facets of the modern FD. The intention is not to be prescriptive, but thought-provoking. All those FDs who are already operating in such an enlightened manner may find that the rest of the text pats them on the back for their vision and skills in a dynamic environment.

5

The FD as general manager

> There are three main qualities I look for in a finance director. They are integrity, a commercial approach and good communication abilities. I take it for granted that a finance director of a major corporation should have wide, general experience, preferably not just in the various financial functions, and enough technical ability, including modern systems, to hold his own internally and externally. (Keith Oates, 1995, Deputy Chairman, Marks & Spencer).

Not so long ago, too many general managers were people who had risen to the top by a process of elimination or attrition. They often adopted a 'macho' style of management. They tended to direct rather than consult. They had often risen through specialist ability or experience and had a scant understanding of finance or information systems. Publications still appear from time to time on the subject of finance for non-financial managers (or directors.) Some directors cry out for an understanding of 'the numbers.' FDs are sometimes jointly culpable in making 'the numbers' seem unintelligible.

All managers should have an acceptable degree of numeracy. All managers should have budgets for which they are accountable. The budget is a quantification of an agreed set of business actions, or a business plan and no manager can adequately understand or account for those actions and plan the consequences without the appropriate level of numeracy.

With financial information increasingly available through intelligent terminals to the manager, there is a joint responsibility on the manager and the finance director to ensure that the necessary skills are available to interpret the information. The FD cannot afford to remain aloof from the whole process.

Above all, a general manager must have an acceptable level of financial awareness and numeracy. While the term general manager might include anyone with a broad ranging senior role in the organisation, a general manager is for this purpose defined as someone in a senior enough position to influence the strategy, direction and implementation of the organisation's business plan. The general manager should also be capable of leading his or her own functional or departmental business plan.

A general manager needs the ability and experience to ask intelligent questions in at least the following areas:

- strategic planning and business development;
- finance;
- marketing;

- information systems;

- human resources, personnel and organisation development.

Any executive director is also a general manager. The finance director is no exception, having a specialist understanding and skills in finance and associated areas (see later), and being increasingly responsible for strategic planning also.

In Geoffrey Owen's *Financial Times* article mentioned earlier, he refers to *The Changing Role of the Finance Director*, (the report from which the table in Chapter 2 has been reproduced). The five most important skills mentioned for the future (in the survey of FDs) were:

- knowledge of information technology;

- personnel management;

- strategic planning;

- marketing;

- general management.

Experience outside finance was considered important, perhaps essential.

> Finance directors are sometimes too remote from the sharp end; a spell in line management has a humbling effect and creates a common bond with colleagues.'A majority agreed that finance directors would become more entrepreneurial. While there were some warning voices, the consensus was that the finance director should not be a technical specialist standing apart from operations, but 'a highly motivated team member dedicated to growing the company'. (Owen, 1995).

Leadership

> I suppose that leadership at one time meant muscle; but today it means getting along with people. (Indira Gandhi).

As well as the above areas of understanding and experience, any director and especially the FD needs to be a leader, entrepreneur, innovator, manager of change and innovation and an excellent communicator. Interpersonal skills of a high order are called for because the FD is dealing with everyone.

Some characteristics of a good leader, in no particular order are:

- clear vision;
- trust;
- high personal standards;
- good self-knowledge;
- listening skills;
- openness and approachability;
- open to ideas;

- integrity;
- strong values;
- ability to set shared goals;
- good interpersonal skills;
- communicator;
- open to a better way;
- consistency and fairness.

Above all, a good leader should empower – someone who creates an environment where the people around them can develop to their full potential.

Backward organisations do not train and develop people. Forward thinking organisations identify the competencies needed to deliver the strategic plan and develop these competencies in their people as far as possible. Leading organisations develop their people, knowing that they are the right people and if they are empowered to develop to the best of their ability, the organisation reaps the harvest and the people feel fully valued to deliver special performance.

All organisations depend on excellence in people, processes and systems. The special factor in any organisation is the people. The key is being clear on the strategy, being flexible and adaptable to change, developing and recruiting the right people and giving them room to perform. That also means giving them scope to make mistakes. This may be difficult for a FD to come to terms with. FDs have been trained in precision. There is a danger of being prescriptive or 'black and white' in one's thinking.

Empowerment and development

A FD who manages through teams, creating the right mix to facilitate understanding, setting and demanding high standards of quality, continuously reviewing performance to learn how to improve, encouraging innovation and entrepreneurship and empowering personal development to maximum potential, is investing heavily in the success of the organisation. Even if people move on to other functions or other organisations, greater performance is achieved from a highly motivated individual feeling they make a recognised contribution to the team. In my experience, the reputation for such a liberated and empowered way of working adds greatly to the ability to recruit and keep able, talented, skilled and committed people.

It should not be necessary to define empowerment. If it exists, everyone will know it. 'As for the best leaders, the people do not notice their existence. The next best, the people honour and praise. The next, people fear, and the next people hate. When the best leader's work is done, the people say "we did it ourselves!".' (Lao-Tzu).

All these things apply to all good leaders. The FD is a leader no less than the MD. They both participate in the strategic leadership of the organisation. The FD leads the financial direction and the finance function and sets an example as much as any manager in the organisation. Above all, the FD is highly visible and, through special skills and understanding of the finances of the organisation, in a position of great actual or potential power for the good of the organisation.

Future prospects

In the aforementioned LBS report, fifty-nine per cent of the seventy-two CFOs interviewed aspired to be CEO in the future. Many FDs succeed in due course to the CEO (or MD's) office. It is highly desirable therefore that they possess the necessary skills, especially general management. Financial skills are fundamental to the success of a MD but leadership is the single most important characteristic.

Although being a capable accountant may not be an indication of being a good manager, even those with limited potential should be given the opportunity to understand what does make a good manager. When the need arises, they will then be able to understand what is the best way forward and take appropriate action. This may involve judgement as to when to seek advice in managing the problem.

Any organisation which has or appoints people into managerial positions has a duty to equip them with the necessary skills or understanding. Britain has been poor at management development in the past. This book is not large enough to explore the enormous possibilities for British industry if we were all trained as global, quality and information oriented, professional, modern managers.

FDs reach the boardroom often by virtue of their financial and accounting skills. They may also have used political or persuasive skills along the way. They have a special responsibility to lead change and liberate the organisation. Too often in the past, financial information has been held (and allowed by others) to be special to the finance people. The duty now is to play a full part as a rounded general manager, a leader, a strategic director, a developer of financial skills in the wider organisation, a liberator of systems and processes (putting the power of the financial information at the fingertips of managers through integrated, networked information systems), providing the necessary advice, guidance and support when called for and developing the people in the finance function to their full potential as team players in the wider organisation. This, above all, will demonstrate the leadership of the FD for the good of the organisation. Then the FD may be ready to aspire to the MD's office.

Culture

The culture of an organisation is critical. A successful organisation's culture would espouse many of the characteristics and values discussed in these pages. Any director must fit in with the culture of the organisation; indeed, will be closely involved in forming it. The FD's importance to the success of the organisation and involvement in the key management processes means that if they are out of line, they can undermine the culture and thereby the commitment of the people. No organisation can profitably afford to have different functions with different cultures. This would be inimical to teamwork, understanding and therefore long term success. A shared culture is based around openness rather than control.

The challenge for the FD is to 'let go', that is to participate in the empowerment of the organisation, facilitating innovation and change for the benefit of all. The FD has fiduciary and governance responsibilities, however. In order for these to be fulfilled, there needs to be an unwritten contract with the rest of the organisation. There might be several elements, such as:

- The FD works to decentralise financial information, so that managers are empowered to make up to the minute, informed, decisions, in return for managers' support for integrated financial systems that allow the FD to report to the corporation as necessary;

- The FD works to facilitate, advise, guide and support managers, as and when required, in the production, use and understanding of financial information, as part of a team where everyone works to promote and improve financial awareness and understanding, throughout the organisation;

- The FD supports financial and budget empowerment of managers, including flexibility as appropriate to facilitate innovation and change, in return for wholehearted participation in an agreed business planning and budgeting process, together with accountability for those plans;

- Finally, each party commits to the principle of 'no surprises' – either way.

Change

Organisations are changing fast. In some, the days of the traditional finance function may be numbered. The finance function is an overhead. If it is not part of the team and the organisation cannot see the incremental value it derives from it, it may now go. In Charles Handy's 'Shamrock' organisation (Handy, 1989) this function may be in the first 'leaf' or the second. Different organisations will come to different conclusions as to what is core business. Already several local authorities have contracted out core functions and disaggregated their management of services into autonomous business units. There is no reason why at least part of the finance function should not go to outside service providers. There are plenty of them. Of course the FD will not be outsourced (except in an interim management situation) but if the information systems and processes are good enough and meet the organisation's requirements, the focus can be on financial advice and guidance with many fewer high quality people, and someone else can do the 'bean counting.'

Tom Peters has referred to Brian Quinn's concept of companies as 'packages of services'. (Quinn, Paquette and Doorley, *Sloan Management Review*, 1990). Peters wrote:

> As service activities assume greater strategic importance, they, like manufacturing activities before them, become candidates for outsourcing. The straightforward advice of Quinn et al was: 'Pursue the best providers of any service and sign them up – before your competitors do.' One needs to ask, activity by activity, are we really competing with the world's best here? If not, can intelligent outsourcing improve our long term. Competitor analysis of service activities should not just consider the company's own industry but should benchmark each service against best in class performance among all service providers... (Peters, 1993).

> Management of change and innovation is probably the most critical and pervasive task facing business and industry today. (William T Brady).

> Having been a Finance Director for some ten years I can confirm that the only constant which I have had to deal with in that period is CHANGE (sic). The extent to which increased competitiveness and technology change have impacted finance has created significant opportunities for finance executives to take a leadership role in their organisations. This has led to a shift away from the traditional comfort

zones of accounting and internal control to the higher ground of strategic planning/competitive advantage, shareholder value, re-engineering activity flows and elimination of non value added tasks. The ability to account for cost is no longer adequate and has been replaced by better understanding of the incidence of cost and establishment of activity/cost drivers. (Mike Smith, 1996, Director, Finance & Information Systems, 3M UK).

Innovation

3M is an organisation in the forefront of innovation. At least twenty-five per cent of its turnover comes from products invented in the previous five years. As I have experienced, too many organisations reject 'off the wall' thinking in order to concentrate on the matter in hand. 3M welcomes lateral thinking and new ideas. Nothing is rejected out of hand.

Innovation, empowerment and problem-solving (or opportunity searching) go hand in hand.

An innovative organisation needs a work force at all levels that has not become so stuck in the rhythm of routine jobs that it cannot easily adapt to a new drumbeat. For change to be a new way of life rather than an occasional traumatizing shock, the Indians as well as the chiefs have to be engaged in change making and change mastery – while still doing their necessary jobs. (Kanter, 1985).

By now it is easy to see why the FD should examine a different way of working. If finance cannot work in the same way as the rest of the culture, it will stand out as a misfit. Whatever the quality of its technical contribution it may not be heard or included. Within the function, opportunities will go begging to make step changes in the contribution of arguably the most important support function. Then, finance will be a prime candidate for outsourcing.

Kanter talks of segmentalism. I talk of 'Box Management'. I have seen too much of it. There are three main types:

- People working in their own boxes – conscientiously, but 'segmented' from the rest of the organisation. They may not even be performing priority tasks, especially if they are not working in a quality way, i.e. understanding their customers' needs and meeting them first time, every time. For the finance function, everyone in the organisation is its customer;

- Seeing everything in different compartments and managing that way. Different people perform different tasks in isolation and sometimes set their own agenda, as opposed to checking the validity against the strategy, prioritising (and eliminating the nice-to-haves) and working in teams for purpose on projects and activities which take the organisation forward;

- The worst type is taking a problem, putting it in a box and either putting the lid on or leaving someone else to sort it out.

It is a maxim in life and in business that every problem is a potential opportunity. The open, team based organisation can decide which to pursue and thereby create opportunities for new products and fresh understanding. Finance cannot afford to be in a box.

Communication

> How many communicators really understand the basic underlying principle of communication? How many well-conceived, well-planned programmes of communication really consist of a one-way stream of information that inundates, and frustrates, and frequently irritates the poor individual on the receiving end? Remember, unless you are receiving as well as transmitting – unless you are getting a playback – you really aren't communicating at all. (Don G Mitchell).

To this, I would add that the prime purpose of communicating is mutual understanding. Anything less is a waste of time. It is a shared process. Many organisations use a top down process. If you do this, you need a continuous, informal audit process to ensure that the message is getting through. However, if you ignore the bottom up feedback of response and new ideas, you will be missing opportunities. This is where flatter, team based organisations score, especially where they are based on fluid teams. The Japanese invest months in understanding so that by the time a product comes to market, for example, they believe they have anticipated any problems. Even then, they never stop listening, to their customers and to their people, and seeking to improve.

Management development

In this chapter I have briefly covered many of the managerial skills and competences that a successful FD should have in the future organisation. These ideas are widely supported in literature, in practice, in anecdote and in dialogue with leaders in finance or their senior colleagues. For many, these skills cannot be acquired overnight. A business degree of some sort, such as an MBA, is a big help, but knowledge and ideas rapidly date. The other ways to effect and maintain management development are to network, listen and discuss, and to read widely. Some will disagree with parts of this book. Different people will have different experiences. It is not intended to be prescriptive – it is meant to be stimulating, thought provoking and enlightening. Many leaders from a wide variety of organisations have contributed up to date thinking to this view of the changing role of the finance director. All refer to a broader role. Many concentrate on the non-financial, broad managerial aspects.

> In today's environment a person has to have the ability to be a rapid reader of outside books, magazines, etc., to keep themselves up to date, and not work on the basis 'I know everything'. (Chairman of a major plc, 1996).

> In a world where middle management is becoming a nomadic occupation, training and retraining is ever more essential. (Robert Bruce, April 1995, *Accountancy*).

In his article, Bruce focused on the work of Sandra Dawson (Peat Marwick Professor of Management Studies, Imperial College London) and the experience of Richard Close (Finance Director of the Post Office). As Dawson noted:

> The world is changing very quickly. The things you learned five years ago will not be relevant any more if you adhere to them strictly...There are individuals who strongly believe they have to take the time to develop their careers and who will make the investment. And there are also companies who want to develop their managers and believe they will keep the managers they train...But the expectation is that individuals will invest in their own training much more than they used to.

And this is even more true today.

Close believes that through management training you can take something like the financial disciplines and embed them elsewhere in the organisation. Once people have their accountancy qualifications then:

we place them elsewhere in the organisation, not necessarily in finance. The scheme has been spectacularly successful. We want the accountants embedded in the processes, not sitting in a sort of accounting factory. It is a question of putting the financial skills into cross-functional groups of people. The term 'accountants' is just shorthand for good finance people.

By now it should not be difficult to see the importance of the finance director's role. It would not be surprising for the FD's role to stand second only to that of MD. Equally, it is no coincidence that many MDs are former FDs. It goes without saying that there should be a close partnership between the two roles (though not to the exclusion of other members of the top team). Their responsibilities are similar, with the FD's expressed in a financial context. Ideally, the MD would present the whole monthly business report to the board, having previously worked through it with the FD and the top team. Consequently there is a need for mutual understanding and trust. Whilst the MD ultimately is accountable for everything the organisation does, he or she has the prime responsibility for leadership of the organisation. The board is entitled to expect that the FD will have a special understanding of the finances and control.

The correct definition of a manager is someone who is responsible for the performance of all the people on whom his own performance depends. (Drucker, 1992).

This includes the boss. The boss is a customer – perhaps your most important customer, especially if you are FD! The key to quality is understanding your customer's needs and meeting them first time every time. With your boss,
the maxim is NO SURPRISES! – especially if you are FD. It is easy to think in terms of 'do as you would be done by'. Each needs to understand the other's strengths and weaknesses. I'm not suggesting sycophancy (although some people make an art of it), just partnership. This means shared understanding, open dialogue and team work (two can be a team and the FD is also a member of the team that the MD leads).

6

The FD as financial manager

In a large international financial services group the finance director must of course have excellent technical skills in finance and accounting. However these are of limited use if he or she does not also have a deep understanding of the business of the group and the markets in which it operates. Objectivity, independence and intellectual honesty are personal qualities which are needed in order that he can give management a clear unbiased view of financial performance and of investment/disinvestment decisions. Modern technology facilitates the cost effective storage of large quantities of data. Today, the finance director should strive to give his company a competitive edge by developing financial information systems which transform this data into relevant information for management decisions about lines of business, products, customers and suppliers, as well as about investment projects and risk assessment. (Sir William Purves, 1995, Group Chairman, HSBC Holdings plc).

Sir William gives an excellent summary of what most people think the core of the role of FD will be for the foreseeable future, irrespective of the need for a broader range of general skills as well.

Management accounting

As we shall see later, the future is about competitive advantage, excellence and benchmarking. In such circumstances, the traditional methods of management accounting appear more likely to hold the organisation back, as techniques such as value based management, balanced business scorecard, or even activity based measures, become more commonplace. The last decade or so has seen the balance shift from recording the past to measuring the present and managing the future. Consequently, management accounting has become a mainstream activity, almost as much as financial accounting. While the methods of scoring past performance for public consumption have come under considerable challenge and are constantly being updated by FRSs and other standards, in pursuit of the elusive 'true and fair view' historic performance becomes of marginal importance when set against the competitive need to 'stay in the game'. What use is a statutory report to shareholders, if the market has just disappeared because you are producing the wrong products, or you are not price competitive?

Books such as *The Goal* and *The Race*, by Eli Goldratt, have asked fundamental questions which could sweep traditional costing methods aside. Once capital equipment has been bought, the cost has gone, so what is the point of seeking to recover overhead if your prices are uncompetitive, or it leads to overproduction in a JIT world? Having been accepted into mainstream accounting, the management accountants now need to transform their thinking or be swept aside by planners and information managers. In an age of added value management, how can the FD as management accountant add sufficient value to justify the overhead of the role? In a 1996 survey in *Management Accounting*, Ernst & Young found that most respondents were interested in speed and efficiency of reporting rather than enhancing the quality of information. What was worrying, apart from this, was that fifty-two per cent of the respondents were FDs or MDs. One of the major areas of difficulty appeared to be in the availability, maintenance and throughput of information systems. Fewer than twenty per cent of the respondents were able to report within five days of the period end.

While management accountants wish to be seen to play a wider role in integrated performance management as part of the strategic processes of the organisation, far more are wishing than doing in this respect. While these feel threatened by the advent of information managers they are either unable or unwilling to change fast enough for this trend to be reversed. If FDs cannot justify their existence on a value added basis, and as active players in the broader team, management may circumvent their purpose except for statutory reasons, or contract out the service need. SMEs often rely on their auditors to supply a value added audit and accounting service until they can afford a full-blown finance function. Accountants with a broad portfolio of clients are becoming more proactive in this respect. What would it take for some organisations simply to wind back the clock and contract out the whole finance function to those with the breadth of experience and vision to carry it out? We shall return to the modern approaches to performance measurement later.

Financial management

While the FD is first and foremost a director, he or she is also expected to possess the skills and experience of a financial manager. In smaller organisations FDs may be involved in the detail of financial management, but in larger organisations, they will usually lead a team and be responsible for the overview.

A good team leader delegates to the team as individual specialists in their area of responsibility. A good FD would have at least understanding and ideally experience in most, if not all, of the relevant areas. Again it often comes down to the ability to ask the right questions, leading and bringing the best out of the team.

Although it may only happen in a crisis, or for a short period, the FD should possess the confidence and the ability to step down into one of the functional roles as necessary e.g. as a result of loss or prolonged absence of a key member of the immediate team. The ideal would be to promote someone temporarily or permanently. In that case, the FD should still be able to coach the new incumbent as appropriate. Sometimes, no-one is available with the relevant skills. The FD would not be expected to let the gap continue to yawn. If it cannot be filled by promotion or reshuffle of the team, the FD can renew his or her understanding in that speciality by temporarily combining it with the more senior responsibilities. It is not desirable for the FD to become gradually more and more aloof from the team members. If the FD is out of touch, how can they quickly spot and rectify a problem?

As financial managers, FDs are not only expected to have the basic skills, ability and qualifications for the role. They should also have either, or preferably both, experience in and an understanding of the key areas. In a small organisation the FD may perform many of these roles, in a larger organisation, he or she will lead the management of:

- management accounting (including forecasting, budgeting, costing, etc.);
- financial accounting (including basic accounting and controls, reporting, systems, processes, etc.);
- financial services (e.g. tax, salaries and wages, debtors and creditors, cash and Treasury accounting, pensions and property accounting, etc.)

Some of the aspects of the role as financial manager are covered in later sections, e.g. treasury management.

In many organisations, there will be standing financial instructions or their equivalent – especially in the public sector. As financial manager, the FD would be expected to recommend these and ensure their implementation, in addition to internal financial control procedures.

Separating the reporting role

As financial manager, the FD will also perform the role of reporting accountant. In the public sector and e.g. the financial services industry, this would include the preparation and submission of statutory accounts and periodic and annual returns.

Financial reporting has an internal dimension as well as an external one. Whilst the FD will manage the preparation of, usually, computer generated internal reports for management and the board, he or she will also be responsible for preparing and often presenting the annual results to shareholders, media, analysts, etc. as appropriate, for quoted companies and other organisations required to have a public meeting. For any registered company, the FD will also have to file annual returns to Companies' House.

In November 1996, David Allen, industrial professor at Loughborough, wrote in *Management Accounting*:

> For some now, the profession has been polarising: some members spend 90-plus per cent of their time on accounting; others spend 90-per cent plus of their time on financial management. The skills required for the two tasks are so different that there are few who are good/happy/effective dividing their time fifty-fifty.

Nevertheless, in this edition, I have recognised this dichotomy by splitting the former chapter on financial management between that and accounting. I shall say less about the latter, because although it is a statutory function of the company, it can be performed outside the organisation. Indeed that, I believe, is the shape of things to come. If there is to be a FD, they should first and foremost be a management accountant, indeed information manager, for the role is a strategic role and so the information provided to management should be strategic.

In a 1996 article in *Management Accounting Research*, Beverley Lord:

> summarised investigations which showed that the various techniques trumpeted as components of strategic management accounting (SMA) were indeed in popular use – but that there was no evidence that the management accounting function ever played any part in them.

Why is this? Are most FDs ostriches, or is it still true that many are stuck in the ways of the past, unable to move from the comfort zone of left brained fact, routine and structure to right brained or better still holistic approaches? I shall leave the last word on this point to David Allen.

> Some very good financial controllers I know are non-accountants; invariably they have a sound grasp of economics, and of the dynamics of the industry in which they are employed. Almost invariably they have an antipathy towards the precision and standardisation of accounting. Are we moving towards the continental approach, where financial management is seen as something quite separate from auditing and accounting? Putting it another way, who in your organisation makes the decisions which determine its financial health? (Allen, 1996).

Adapt or die! What is the value of financial information which is meaningless or unintelligible to management in a fast-changing highly competitive world, worse still if it is also weeks out of date?

Financial information for management

David Jacobs says:

> there are two important elements in remaining in control as a manager: the need to have up-to-date financial and non-financial data in a form which is meaningful to operating managers; and the need to involve as many managers as possible in the analysis and interpretation of results. Managers need monthly financial reports. The essence of any control system is comparing actual results with desired results, and, if necessary, taking immediate corrective action. (Jacobs, 1991).

Good financial and other information reflects the up to date performance of the organisation. While benchmarking is now in vogue (see Chapter 16), the best performance indicators will be those which succinctly and accurately measure the specific performance of the organisation against its own predetermined targets and plans. Drucker identifies five sets of measurement of the overall performance of a company:

- market standing;
- innovative performance;
- productivity;
- liquidity and cash flows;
- profitability.

(Drucker, 1992).

The FD would be involved in producing most of this information. Note the importance of cash flow. I would add key customer measures. Some corporations have hundreds! If there are more than a few, they are not key. This is a topic which will be dealt with later.

While Drucker's measures would do well for most companies, there would be variations for different organisations, especially non-profit or public sector organisations. These are not expected to make a profit, but they are expected to at least break even on a recurring basis. All have to manage cash tightly and many have to demonstrate publicly a return on capital employed. All organisations should have measures of quality built into their overall appraisal, especially service organisations.

Whatever the organisation, some of the measures will be financial in nature. All organisations should be accountable for the use of the funds provided, whatever the source. A quoted company may determine returns on capital invested in it. This would also be appropriate to a NHS trust which might also look at productivity, capacity usage, etc as well as an in-year balanced budget. A school or university also needs to balance the books but would focus on academic success rates. A charity would be concerned about the success of fund raising.

In an era where quality rules, and constant innovation is necessary to stay ahead of the rest of the pack, financial measures alone are not sufficient to gauge the health and vitality of the organisation. If the focus is mainly on financial measures, there is a danger of tending towards financially based remedies. In the public sector, there has been a tradition of cutting costs when the books do not balance. Nothing is more demotivating to a good manager. In any organisation, if there is a culture of red-lining costs, there will also be people who cheat in the budgetary process, either creating hidden contingencies to manage cost overruns, or inflating draft budget proposals in the knowledge that when the inevitable 5% is removed, the budget will remain manageable. This is the problem of money based plans and measures of performance. As is discussed later, plans and budgets should be based around activities, including understanding cost drivers.

Performance measurement

For me, the most important measures relate to customers, the cash value of the business, the value added by the management and business processes and those relating to quality of people and processes. On this latter point, the biggest falsehood in the annual reports of observed business is 'our people are our greatest asset'. They are certainly the greatest cost, even now, in a largely service-oriented economy, but judging by the stressed-out state of the nation, they do not feel like the most important asset. Yet, in a 1998 survey by Sheffield University's Industrial Psychology unit, Michael West reported that by far the biggest factor in differentiating competitive performance in a range of UK industrial companies was through HR practices (seventeen per cent of all reported instances). Since the first edition of this book, many people have approached me to say that it is the people element which is most sadly neglected in the policies, presentations and practices of the accountancy bodies.

One possible way forward for overall performance measurement to capture a holistic view is the use of a 'balanced scorecard' approach. As Rod Newing wrote in November 1994 in *Accountancy*, 'companies like Apple, Intel, Brown & Root and NatWest are using balanced scorecards to manage in a way that integrates traditional financial measures with operational and softer customer and staff issues, which are vital to long term competitiveness'. As Robert Kaplan (Harvard Business School) has said, ' the balanced scorecard starts with the view that the overall goal of a corporation is to generate long term economic value'. (Kaplan, 1995). In the two years since the first edition, the professional press has taken up BBS and VA, VBM approaches to performance measurement as if they were the norm that they should be.

Planning and accounting for long term value

Long term economic value or shareholder value is now the key financial target for many companies. This has been a major development in recent years. The theory has been around for a very long time. Not only has it now become the prime focus, but there have also been three other key developments for the FD to factor into strategic planning, direction and performance measures. The first is the move towards measuring a company's worth in terms of cashflows as opposed to earnings per share. The second is the change in both political focus and economic reality towards low inflation on a global basis. The third is the widespread move towards determining the economic value added through the processes during a chosen period for an organisation.

Low inflation policies have largely resulted from the shocks and fallout of the two recent major oil crises and the consequent failure of economic policy in a raft of economies worldwide (starting with Britain's recourse to the IMF in the 1970s). All major economies are now pursuing a policy of managed, sustainable growth with low inflation. This would return us to the relative stability last experienced in the 1950s and 1960s.

The trouble is that with most of management, FDs, speculators, investors, politicians, having pursued their careers since that era, it takes some getting used to and trusting. The consequence is an irrational fear of resurgent inflation and a probable tendency to overreact. In the early 1980s when I was a stockbroker, I remember being shocked when the ticker tape showed a 20 point move in the FT Index in one day. Since then we have had 200 point plus moves and 50 points either way in the same day is not unusual. In the 1960s, inflation and interest rates were low, predictable and manageable and volatility was low. Now we have returned to low rates but volatility is greater.

Volatility is partly a product of global influences in markets. FDs have new tools to cope with volatility e.g. futures and other hedging instruments. Companies like to increase the predictability of performance in the short term and these tools help to fix costs, currencies and interest rates, especially when the company is operating, buying or selling in international markets. Very little is immune from global influences. While company and industry-specific factors can affect relative performance of shares, global factors can induce quite substantial absolute changes. These can make it difficult to plan the long term cost of capital. It used to be said that 'if America sneezes the world catches a cold'. Now it seems that international stock markets mirror Wall Street's performance. Whatever our domestic influences, the level of our interest rates must reflect what is happening in the US and Europe. Global bond markets dictate the price of money.

There is much debate about the level of target rates of return and FDs have been criticised for leaving these in some cases at twenty per cent or more when inflation and interest rates are now consistently low figures. Policy makers are concerned about the implications for investment and employment. Although it is likely that these target rates will come down slowly as confidence grows, the main reason for the high levels is the greater focus on, and incidence of risk in, global markets, where the pace of innovation and technological change can lead to rapid erosion of competitive advantage. If payback periods must be shorter, then rates of return will remain high in real terms. The job of the FD is not to explain things away, however, but to work with management to increase efficiency and productivity and invest in innovation in order to sustain value.

Measuring performance in a low inflation era

Emerging markets have increased the strength of competition in this new low inflation era. The needs for steady growth in efficiency are being driven by shrinking margins. Overseas competitors will push up the price of raw materials, but they have lower wage costs. Consumers are not prepared to pay steadily inflating prices and so margins are under pressure. The most significant characteristic of the last recession was that large numbers of middle managers lost their jobs. That has been a once off saving. Now productivity and innovation must take the strain.

Accountants have struggled for two decades to decide how to account for inflation. Now the burden has been removed. The problem was that appreciating commodity and asset prices could give a false idea of the performance of a company. In some cases they saved bad management from paper losses. For companies the price/earnings ratio became an illusion, because there were so many different factors unique to individual companies and so many ways of measuring earnings that this has become an unreliable measure. This in part explains the volatility of earnings and encourages a more short-termist outlook. Each profits warning is followed by an immediate savaging of the share price.

Indeed, in my view, the single biggest practical problem for companies is the short-termist attitude which is more prevalent in the UK than in any other economy in the world. It is no wonder that TQM has been abandoned or deemed not to work here, when it so obviously still works in the leading economies of the world. TQM and other quality based approaches require at least medium and often long term commitment in order to deliver benchmark performance. Indeed they need fundamental culture change.

Value added

Every company does it, but measuring performance has no meaning without a context, whether it be past performance, relative to competitors or peers, or especially benchmark performance. The successful FD of tomorrow will lead the strategic processes and therefore needs strategic measures of performance. The past, or lagging indicators are a waste of time in the dynamic global economies which are now the norm. EPS and ROI do not measure the potential for future cash-generation which is the modern currency of performance. If we continue to be short-termist, we may penalise ourselves by using historic, outdated, misleading measures which lead to uncertainty of capital-raising in increasingly innovation driven markets. Shareholder value driven approaches based on ridiculous discount factors need to be replaced by shareholder value analysis (SVA) and economic value added (EVA) type methods. EVA, referred to later, is a trade mark of Stern Stewart.

However, it is not easy to change current practice, despite the obvious advantages. Companies fail through running out of cash. (Look at Polly Peck, which remained highly 'profitable' to the last minute.) They could have reasonable historic EPS performance and still find themselves insolvent. The Japanese use a mix of measures combining market share, profitability and innovation. There is too much vested interest in the financial community in using traditional accounting measures and intransigence in the investment community where the proliferation of standards may have improved the standard of accounting, but have added to the meaningless absolute and relative comparisons of reported performance.

So what can we do instead? The FDs can take the lead. If I could have one wish for the outcome of this book, it would be to achieve lasting change in all the key aspects I have covered. I hope it will be read by all kinds of general managers for its general messages, rather than just by FDs (unless the latter succeed in championing change). The UK once again has the opportunity to lead the world, in the 21st century.

The finance community has come up with ABC, ABCM and ABM; and the US produced EVA, which is a better measure of the long-term use of capital. TQM, CSF and KPI have survived to underpin the balanced scorecard devised by Kaplan and Norton, which is based on four aspects of a business: customers, internal capability, innovation, and shareholders (broadened to stakeholders where appropriate). We shall return to the BBS.

So if the FD will find historic accounting more certain in the low inflation environment, financial management and planning will become even harder and the balance has swung through management accounting to information management (the now and the future). For this reason and the evolution of the FD's role, there is now a separate chapter later on information management. Maybe this is the core role for the FD of tomorrow. Cashflow will be more important than earnings and will increasingly be used to measure the net present value of the corporation.

Balanced scorecard (BBS)

Performance measures are a means for translating the theory of strategy into the practicalities of implementation. 'What you measure you achieve.' Balanced scorecards cover the full range of key issues: customers, innovation, internal processes and financial. The approach continues to evolve. It has long been recognised that a mix of financial and non-financial indicators gave a better balance of overall performance, but one of the criticisms was the subjectivity of the latter measures. Meanwhile, in Japan, the link between management accounting and strategy has avoided the possibility that traditional accounting and taxation factors can blur the understanding of overall performance. Forward thinking FDs have embraced techniques which overcome the potentially stultifying effects of standard costing.

Activity based costing (ABC, or ABCM) was the first major step on the road to a better recognition of 'true' cost, but as process management has achieved acceptance, ABM (activity based management) has become more relevant. The FD has moved from understanding cost drivers to activity drivers, not just costs, but especially quality, response times and innovation. When you start to analyse the cost drivers, they suggest several worthwhile non-financial measures also.

We have discussed the costs of quality elsewhere. Again, there are several worthwhile non-financial quality measures, e.g. customer retention, repeat orders, customer complaints, returned goods, etc. When we come to time based measures we see fundamental change in the focus of the FD. Returning to Goldratt's books, the modern preoccupation is with throughput accounting (TA), rather than utilisation, productivity, efficiency and achieving budget. Recent surveys consistently suggest that time-based measures are most significant: fast and reliable delivery and speed of design change. The balanced scorecard asks the following questions: what do our stakeholders expect; what do our customers expect; what must we be excellent at (e.g. benchmarked against the 'best of the best'); and how can we create added value and continuously improve our processes? Which leads us to value based approaches.

Measuring and managing long term shareholder value

Among the key aspects of a finance director's job identified by the chief executive of one of the major electricity companies in the UK are: 'contributing to the strategic development of the company in its efforts to grow shareholder value; financing the company's operations and development in a way which optimises the combination of total return to shareholders and risk management; and producing early and accurate management information which helps line managers to perform better – i.e. it is tailored to the manager's needs rather than the accountant's needs.'

For non-profit organisations, this would be stakeholder value and bring into play a more subjective analysis. However, even for companies, value is not just measured in financial terms. For customers it is to do with satisfying their needs. Success will be measured in the longevity of and gains from the customer relationship. This is particularly important in financial services organisations, where pricing and margins can be calculated from relatively accurate NPV projections, product by product.

For employees there are many ways of feeling valued, ranging from tangible rewards to training and development and other intangible forms of recognition. For shareholders, the value is in the dividends and the share price performance. In the UK, share prices are still largely influenced by earnings projections. In the US and increasingly in the UK, projections of cashflow are more frequently being adopted.

> Studies of market behaviour show that shareholders invest on the business's ability to generate long term cash flows with the level of return expected dependent on the level of risk. Yet, many companies continue to focus on earnings. (Richard Barfield, March 1994, *Professional Manager*).

> Anyone who still uses earnings per share needs his head examining. (David Tweedie, 1994, Chairman of the Accounting Standards Board).

There are many problems with an FD relying on earnings. Various factors can affect the earnings figure, making it unreliable for inter company or year on year comparison. The effects of inflation mentioned earlier have been a problem in the past and some of the companies which failed in the late 1980s and early 1990s cannot have been helped by focusing on earnings growth rather than value creation. The former is too much of a financial measure. The latter is more of a corporate measure of all round performance.

Different practices for accounting for acquisitions, provisioning, depreciation, valuation of assets, etc. have complicated matters in the past. It should also be borne in mind that it is lack of cash rather than lack of capital which bankrupts companies (although the latter can contribute to the former.) It was no surprise that the regional electricity companies generated such huge predatory interest from US companies because they are 'cash cows'. Cash flow is critical to some companies. Earnings can give a false feeling of comfort.

One of the key aspects of the FD's role for Brian Wilson is 'to ensure the strategic vision of the company is underpinned by the reality of proper investment appraisal and the importance of cash'. (Wilson, 1995, Finance Director, Norweb plc).

Value based management

Once the FD thinks in terms of cash-generation and added value (whether short or long term), many questions come to mind. This book does not always offer answers. The economic world is constantly evolving and alert FDs will know the questions to ask for their own organisation. VBM is largely based around measures such as EVA and SVA (economic and strategic value added), CFROI (cash flow return on investment), TSR (total shareholder return), and NPV (net present value).

I do not propose to embark on a discourse on each, other than to make the general point of their relevance to a customer oriented, fast changing, competitive global marketplace. In such a marketplace, EPS, standard costing and traditional measures, such as ROC, will not survive, except alongside inefficiency and underperformance. Traditional FDs have held or exercised too much power for too long, through the mystique of accounting and reporting. To be fair, managers have been compliant in this plot by refusing or failing to understand the language and techniques. Now, spurred on by a wave of MBAs and the harsh reality of the marketplace, they demand to know what really counts.

FDs can still add value across the range of faculties described in this book, but their best duty will be in playing in the broad team as facilitators of understanding. That way the managers will own the business and, properly communicated, the breadth of financial and non-financial measures can lead to better understanding, involvement and motivation for all employees. Added value is something that the person on the Clapham bus can appreciate. Semivariable overheads are not. The loss of their job when the company goes bust due to loss of markets, overproduction, failure to adapt, downsizing and running out of cash, they can understand.

VBM links financial and non-financial measures to corporate strategy in a real and meaningful way. The process of value analysis starts by determining such things as what enriches cashflow and creates long term value. What are the value drivers – customer acquisition and retention, innovation, long term sales growth, margins and sound investments, etc.? What are the critical success factors (CSFs) from the perspective of the various stakeholders? What are the key performance indicators at strategic and operating level (KPIs)?

Economic value management (EVM/EVA/SVA)

I have regretted elsewhere the apparent demise of TQM. While it is alive and well in the Far East (and in parts of North America), as a way of life it has been dismissed by too many in the UK as another passing fad. Why? Because many were not committed to the long term and the investment it would take, and management changes too often. Without a market imperfection, only quality companies should survive in the 21st century. That means being largely customer-focused and preoccupied with excellence of people, processes and systems, together with continuous improvement and innovation and lifetime learning.

VBM brings together TQM, EVM, BBS and the customer focus. ABM and ABCM will ensure better understanding of what really drives performance, and will also inform the continuous need for organisational change. Go back to read what Hammer and Champy really said about BPR, because, together with an ABM approach, the FD can facilitate real changes in efficiency, improved effectiveness, better service levels *and* lower costs.

One of the major misunderstandings by management has been to try and use techniques in isolation under the guidance of one guru or another. They fit together as a set. If there is one message that Goldratt conveys in all his books, it is 'think about everything you are doing'. That is why slavish adherence to the routine production of historic accounting information could spell disaster to the corporation and the traditional role of the FD.

Routine, periodical reporting of an organisation's performance, internally and externally, will always be a part of the FD's role and the format of statutory and regulatory reports will be set by outside authorities and augmented by the accountancy bodies. All other performance information produced by the FD must be meaningful and relevant, otherwise it is a waste of time. Furthermore, information will be required faster. Even if a report is produced within three days of a month end, elements of that information will be up to a month out of date. In addition, if managers receiving the figures are reactive, this diminishes its value further.

Good managers have an instinctive and informed understanding of what is happening in their part of the business. The figures do not come as a surprise, unless there is an error. By the time a variance is revealed, the good manager knows the reason and has already commenced remedial action. The poor manager will find out there is a problem from the monthly report and by the time action has been taken, two to three months could have been lost. Ideally there will be a partnership between the FD and the rest of management to ensure that they get the information they need to gauge the key performance of the enterprise and take corrective action where necessary. Financial measures are only worthwhile if they lead to better quality decisions and are relevant to the agreed goals and strategy.

Economic value added (EVA)

EVA is a trade mark concept developed by Stern Stuart, who have introduced it to hundreds of clients in the US and some in the UK. Price Waterhouse took the concept further in their book *In Search of Shareholder Value: Managing the Drivers of Performance*, 1997. Two powerful strands are pulling these new techniques of measuring corporate performance: the need to move away from unreliable and inconsistent earnings per share measures, including to cash-based measures; and the global focus on shareholder value. It is said that even the Japanese may be moving in the latter direction. If this is to be a global trend, I see upsides and downsides.

It must be right to find ways to measure business performance on a cash value or generation basis, provided the effects of major capital decisions can be smoothed out. Furthermore, any metric which allows a common standard of comparison between quoted and unquoted companies, manufacturing and service companies, has much to commend it. I still worry about the likely increased trend to short-termism, which must eventually override long-term value creation and economic stability. It is inevitable that if management's focus is increasingly short term, then performance, shares and markets will be more volatile. This will be exacerbated if the 'no-brain' decision of selling off or closing operations and returning cash to shareholders continues to grow – and I do not see signs of a reverse.

EVA is already encouraging the acquisition of more debt instead of equity and I can see the financial arguments in favour of that, but in a net nil gain world, increased tax-deductions for debt must be balanced somewhere. Furthermore, while debt and equity ultimately draw from the same world pond, there must be an absolute and a relative appetite for debt, and supply and demand factors will eventually establish themselves. In the meantime, EVA has a sound basis in estimating the net gain in value of the corporation in a financial period. That is a common currency that everyone from the boardroom to the shop floor can understand, especially if they are rewarded on such a common basis too. Provided that the balanced scorecard approach is used to focus the drivers of the economic value, it may be that the short term can be balanced with the long term.

Terry Smith has done much to debunk the mystique, confusion and distortion of corporate financial information. In the process, he lost his job as an analyst and made a reputation as a financial commentator and author. He unearthed confusing and misleading information in reported corporate profits. What worries me about SVA is that a central part of its calculation is post tax profit. Profit is also at the heart of earnings per share. Stern Stuart themselves admit to making up to 164 adjustments in arriving at EVA. While the concept is simple, the calculation is not and unless we are to have e.g. a Yellow Book or treasury enforced standard for calculation, we may run into the same problems and be at the mercy of a select group of analysts. That is why, although I applaud anything which moves away from EPS and the poor investments which have been made by relying on it, like Warren Buffett, I prefer cash as a common currency.

Profit and costs

Traditionally, one of the aspects of the FD's role would have been to control costs in the organisation. Certainly the FD or equivalent would be expected to take the lead in the public sector, for example. As implied elsewhere, it should now be understood that costs are the responsibility of everyone in the organisation. This would not relieve the expectation that the finance function should be able to facilitate the management of costs.

Costing was a traditional skill taught to most accountants. The principles of, for example, standard costing and variance analysis would be fundamental to the FD's role in many organisations, especially manufacturing. When a new product was designed and put into production, each element was precisely costed in order, for example to determine the selling price. Problems started to appear, however, once it was necessary to determine how to allocate or apportion overhead to each product. Costs are partly a function of volume and we now realise that time is a key element in costing (especially when storage or transportation are taken into account.)

I do not propose to embark on a detailed treatise on cost accounting for two reasons: first, because that is not the purpose of this book; and, second, because attitudes to the evaluation and management of costs have changed. Drucker even sees profit as a cost (Drucker, 1992). If the financial purpose of an organisation is to maximise long term stakeholder value, then profit can be seen as a cost. Some examples will clarify the point:

- In a company, profit is for two purposes: first to remunerate the owners of the business (e.g. dividends to shareholders); and second to provide for future capital investment (the cost of capital). In both cases, there is a cost. If the profits generated are too much for those purposes, then a number of things may happen. First, the dividend may be increased by more than expected. Second, cash may be returned to shareholders in special dividends, scrip issues, share buybacks, etc. If cash still accumulates, in excess of the company's needs, it may be vulnerable to takeover by another company which can put the cash to better use;

- In a non-profit making organisation, profits or surpluses are also a cost. Again, retained cash may be invested in capital goods, or may be returned to purchasers in the form of lower prices until the surplus is used up.

All costs are the result of business decisions and actions. To cut costs means cutting activities. The question is, if it is possible to cut costs, is it necessary to undertake the activities in the first place. Organisations are taking an increasingly strong line on activities that do not add value. This does not necessarily mean that all 'discretionary' activities are cut out. It does mean, however, that after all 'necessary' activities have been agreed, the organisation is able to choose whether to spend money on other things, such as community projects or sponsorship.

The FD's role in cost management is to lead and facilitate the process. The FD's impartiality means that he or she can constructively challenge the level of costs in any part of the enterprise. This does not apply to the costs of the finance function itself. This function should only be sufficient to perform those tasks and roles that management see as adding value. As mentioned earlier, the finance function is an overhead. It is relatively straightforward to determine what is mandatory, what is desirable and what is 'nice to have' in any budget. One assumes these days that the 'nice to haves' do not survive. Costs can be prioritised and once the necessary costs of core activities have been taken into account, the line of affordability usually falls somewhere in the desirable activities. Here, different interests will compete to make their case.

Strategic review of costs

The above is a somewhat simplistic way of looking at the matter of budgeting. The FD can use a number of approaches to challenge the necessity and affordability of different activities (which have a consequential cost). At the time of strategic review, it is important to agree what is core and non-core. There should be more discretion and flexibility over non-core activities. By that I mean that questions may be asked about these, such as:

- Do we need to do this?

- Do we need to do it this way?

- How can we do it another way and achieve the same end at lower cost?

One of the major developments in this latter respect is the increasing tendency to outsource non-core activities (assuming they are agreed as necessary to support the core). The growing prevalence of flatter organisations and slimmer head offices is testimony to growing economies in non-core activities.

Non-core businesses can be demerged, sold off, subjected to management buy-outs, etc. A growing practice for non-core activities is to make the providers redundant, give them a lump sum to establish themselves as commercial entities and contract for, say, half their annual activity. This is an approach used by Rank Xerox and others. A FD could of course put the finance function out to tender except for a high quality core of specialists and internal consultants, but it is not necessary to do this to demonstrate the FD's impartiality.

Other questions in the strategic review might include:

- How are we organised?

- Is this optimal to deliver all our purposes?

- Are the management and business processes exactly what we need to deliver the plan and afford an agreed degree of flexibility for change?

- Does the information strategy match the organisation and business strategy? Does it provide only the information management needs, cost-effectively and at the time it is needed?

If the cost level is still too high to deliver the necessary level of profit, it may be necessary to look at marginal businesses and their interdependence. Having prioritised their importance in terms of contribution to profitability, they could be incrementally divested until the overall target return on capital (i.e. profit) can be achieved (provided that divestment does not damage the core business). Sometimes this may mean revisiting the questions of 'what business are we in?' and 'what is core?'

At the time of budgeting the FD should lead a process of activity based or zero based budgeting as the optimum way to ensure that costs reflect only the activities that are agreed as necessary to achieve the overall agreed purpose. The basis of activity based management is to understand the critical activities of the business. For each discrete operation and for the corporation as a whole, these will usually be only a handful of high level processes. An understanding of the outputs required from each process, the inputs necessary to achieve those outputs and the cost drivers, rapidly and effectively enables management to understand what the core activities really are and the cost and profitability of those activities. Too many organisations have undertaken a business process re-engineering approach to achieve one-off cost savings. A better solution is to use an ongoing ABM approach so that the necessity and cost-effectiveness of key processes are always under review

Costs are a function of profit. The reason for profits has been identified earlier, i.e. to remunerate capital (especially shareholders). If costs are too high, another way of looking at it is that profits are too low. Before cutting into the core to balance the books the FD should ask whether capital needs are too high. Or, whether a different capital mix would achieve the same objectives at a lower average cost (and therefore lower need for profit resulting in more tolerance for cost).

One way to do this is to look at the sources of finance (e.g. borrowing, hire, purchase, etc.) and the gearing of capital funds. Provided that the FD is satisfied that the organisation's costs are no more than are necessary to deliver the agreed objectives, then ways to cope with that level of cost are worth exploring. If costs are still too high (i.e. profits too low), the problem may become one of managing the confidence level of stakeholders (shareholders, customers, staff, funders, sponsors, etc.) who may choose to move their support elsewhere. One glance at the effects of profit warnings by companies on the price of their quoted shares in recent years is ample justification for managing costs tightly and optimally, together with the expectations of stakeholders. This latter relationship management is also part of the FD's role (see Chapter 15).

Modern approaches to costing and budgeting

We have touched on activity based methods, but in keeping with the focus on quality, which is a key theme of this book, it is also appropriate to touch on target costing and other approaches. The traditional costing method was based on cost-plus, but while I have deliberately put that in the past tense, there is still a substantial proportion of manufacturing industry which uses this method. Any method which is based on absorption is fraught in the fast changing markets of today. It could also lead to organisations deluding themselves that they are efficient by using capital assets way beyond their 'sell-by' date. Goldratt would not be alone in wanting to know about wastage rates, retooling time, breakdowns and delays, speed of production, inflexibility of product or component change, etc. Furthermore, in such a regime, companies may not be planning the financial consequences of re-equipping and an inflexible approach to manufacture can be carried through to the attitude to stakeholders, especially customers and employees, both of whom will personally experience the consequences of quality failures and obsolescence.

Target costing was first introduced by Toyota in the 1960s and is increasingly regarded as reflecting the real world. It is a matter of looking down the right end of the telescope. Accountants may tell you the barrel is half empty. Marketeers will tell you it is half full.

An accountant may start by adding up the variable costs and adding elements of fixed costs to ensure full recovery of overhead. A profit margin completes the sum of a cost plus price. The product may sell a certain quantity in the market place. The target cost approach starts with an understanding of the market place, customer needs, competitive products and the possibility of added value features. A price is determined which will 'clear the market' based on volume demand expectations and product life cycle expectations. The required profit margin is deducted to arrive at the target cost. Review of all the processes and every aspect of production then determines how the product can be produced for the given level of demand, at the right specification and quality standard, to the delivery requirements. Using this approach, it is often amazing what improvements can be achieved to meet the requirement.

Standard costing

So is standard costing dead? In an excellent article in *Management Accounting* (April 1997), Mike Lucas argued the pros and cons of standard costing. Arrayed against it were all the features of 'strategic manufacturing' which will be recognised from the quality, process, continuous improvement arguments in the present book. In a JIT, advanced manufacturing techniques (AMT), TQM world, six different examples were given for the inappropriateness, irrelevance or limitations of standard costing. The arguments were highly persuasive. When it came to putting forward the arguments in favour, these were largely about how standard costing could be adapted to the modern environment. The main basis for retaining standard costs was where Kaizen was used alongside target costing, requiring interyear comparison of costs to measure improvement.

While this may be valid, it does not change my own conclusion that it is time to move on, in a customer and quality oriented world. There are two approaches to overheads: seek to recover them through a standard costing based approach, or, reduce them, stop them, or do not incur them in the first place. If my prediction of a total quality, continuous improvement, customer driven global market in the 21st century is true (if this is not already the case), then rigid adherence by the FD to traditional costing methodologies may lead to the FD's overhead being questioned!

Budgeting

The next question is what is the future for budgeting? I have outlined a rational planning cycle earlier, but I have also made clear that, in a rapidly changing world, the strategic plan must remain flexible. For many organisations an annual planning and budgeting process focuses the mind on the challenges, opportunities, needs and risks, and also helps to meet the strict demands of a higher authority, e.g. the government in the public sector, through the public spending round.

Equally, for a substantial and growing number of companies the budgeting process may be an anachronism, and at the very least is confusing to management and employees or at worst, too restrictive to allow the necessary flexibility to adjust to constantly changing market conditions. Most especially, a budget will be based on a fixed set of assumptions, which, as well as being arbitrary, are made at a fixed point in time, often on the basis of historical information and sometimes outdated and irrelevant before the budget comes into effect. Even organisations which are quite good at budgeting may fix budgets based on the previous year and given reporting timetables, the budget may not be agreed until well into the period for which it relates. As illustrated elsewhere, the further into the budget period a variance occurs, the more it costs pro rata to recover the targeted level.

In my experience to budget properly takes a huge amount of every manager's time. Given the natural human expectation that budgets will get pared back, some managers will always inflate budgets. Those who do not eventually get penalised when they also get pared back. Without adequate financial sophistication, managers will work on the best available information and therefore, traditionally, budgets will be 'bottom up' like traditional costing. Many organisations have abandoned budgeting, e.g. IKEA in 1992.

In my own experience, budgeting can be very useful for challenging expenditure, especially overhead, in the public sector. For it to be rational, however, the manager preparing a budget must have a first class understanding of the business as must whoever is challenging the budget, e.g. the FD. Otherwise it can be almost a pointless exercise. Of course the public sector will always have to live within spending constraints, but in an ideal world, managers will have a shared understanding of the organisation's targets and, working to deliver these, will be allocated an agreed amount of money to spend as they see fit in delivering those targets. This is more or less the approach used where local authorities and NHS trusts have disaggregated into self-managing units, with the added flexibility of being able to generate income to mitigate net costs.

In the private sector, the idea of the FD telling managers how much they can spend seems somewhat passé. With leading edge organisations managing across processes, rather than up and down functional 'chimneys', and with the most critical targets being related to customers, through a balanced scorecard, towards benchmark performance in an empowered environment, budgeting seems somewhat restrictive and bureaucratic.

If the organisation of the 21st century is to be managed holistically, through flexible adaptable processes, then budgeting no longer fits. It seems tied up with a short-term, cost-cutting, downsizing, 'black hole' mentality which could lead to the progressive shrinking of corporations and repayment of share capital, as opposed to the TQM, stakeholder-led, value-added, process-based costing, long-term value creation, benchmarked company of the future. Budgeting always felt authoritarian, rather than participative and whenever the red pen is wielded the old attitudes will be reinforced.

Financial services

There are many challenges for the FD of the future, not least the growing spread of responsibilities. While the role should become more one of a general manager, as senior financial manager the FD will still be called on to lead the financial management processes, whether or not they are contracted out. So much of the traditional role of the FD has been routine. When a company starts out in business, it can neither justify nor afford the cost of a FD. The financial processes will often be wholly contracted to a firm of accountants, who also do the audit, pay the salaries and often may collect and pay the bills. At some stage the company decides that it wishes to take these processes in-house. Software packages and platforms to perform all the financial services are now readily available, relatively cheap and largely homogeneous. For a complex organisation, it may be cost-effective either to manage such services centrally, disaggregate them into the subsidiary businesses, or contract them out.

In an age where we should be increasingly preoccupied with a business focus, largely centred around the customer, we should be asking:

- What is our core business?

- What do we need to do to achieve our corporate goals?

- What is the most efficient set of processes to do this?

- What do we not need to do, while still being able to deliver?

Support services must be an aspect which is called into question. Some years ago, I forecast that the support services industry (including IT/IS, financial and management services), would see compounded real income growth of at least ten per cent per annum. Since that time, companies like SEMA and SERCO have grown from fledglings to substantial corporations. My forecast was undercast. As we shall discuss later, every support function can be outsourced. If you were building your business from scratch today, would you really need to have all the support functions, with the complexity and inefficiency of corporate communications, or would you prefer to design a business whose business processes were wholly dedicated to determining and meeting customers' needs, building and capitalising on a brand? That is the basis of the virtual corporation. There may be no time in the 21st century to do it any other way.

As I have stressed, this book is not a 'how to' textbook. The FD will still be responsible for accounts payable, accounts receivable, salaries, PAYE, NHI, VAT, etc. As FD, would you choose to do these things directly, or, with the growing spread of responsibilities, would you be better contracting these out and focusing on the strategic, value added aspects of the role? What should your colleagues expect you to be doing – reconciling the salaries control account, or worrying about the critical strategic challenges of EMU, year 2000 and derivatives. We shall move on.

EMU

EMU is largely covered under treasury management, but, as with year 2000, this is an area which virtually no FD can ignore. We may not enter the new single currency until well into the next century, but in the meantime, many of our suppliers and customers in Europe will transact and invoice in Euros. This will bring new currency management, financial management, marketing and information systems challenges right now.

Although year 2000 will be the most pressing single problem facing most businesses until well into the said year, EMU cannot be put on the back burner. If you are going to have to change your financial systems for year 2000 compatibility, ideally you would make sure that they are capable of accounting in Euros, as soon as possible. Your colleagues will not thank you for demanding more capital budget for the latter. The consequences of implementing two system modifications concurrently are far less than sequentially and especially, the overall risk of error will be relatively less. However, the high risk of failing to meet year 2000 compliance is so great that some organisations may decide to implement the two changes separately. This is likely to put them at a severe competitive disadvantage after EMU starts.

Pensions management

This is an area FDs cannot afford. This is not to say that the FD should manage either the funds management process or the payment systems. These can be readily contracted out to specialist providers. The more pressing question, following Maxwell, Greenbury and other recent developments is how you manage for the consequences of pensions in an environment where so much change is taking place. A final salary pension is still one of the major benefits an employer can offer. Whether you adopt the IASC or ASB approach, the financial consequences which the FD must take into account are constantly fluctuating, for a number of reasons. The questions to be asked, are:

- Does the company offer a pension scheme, or does it rely on personal pension provision?

- What is the most appropriate method to value the incremental change in liability for a particular year, in order to account on both a true and fair and prudent basis?

- Should the fund be managed in-house, contracted out or should a tracker or similar fund be used?

The Chancellor's decision to abolish ACT in the 1998 budget will accelerate the move away from company pensions, when taken in conjunction with the other important factors. With more employers offering a menu based approach, it is easier, probably less expensive and certainly less fraught to encourage employees to set up personal pension arrangements, whether or not the company contributes, or simply pays a higher salary to compensate.

In the good old days, companies occasionally had a pensions 'holiday' which boosted corporate profits for that particular year. With the growing impact of volatile markets, transfers of contributions, redundancy and early retirement, the financial accounting consequences are becoming much more fraught. Now, we have the Greenbury inspired requirement for the incremental value of directors' accumulated rights to be valued and accounted for each year. Furthermore, whether or not IASC and ASB concur on the accounting for pensions, there remains an element of subjectivity at a time when both employers and employees have moved towards growing flexibility of contract.

The three main ways of purchasing a pension have been through money purchase, private purchase and managed funds. In the latter case, statistics cannot be overridden. If half pension managers are outperforming the market index, then half are underperforming. Furthermore, tracker funds are not the obvious answer, because costs mean that a tracker fund cannot perform better than the index it is tracking. Why not pass the decision and risk to an employee who has been made less secure by shortening terms of contract and institutionalised downsizing?

Meanwhile, with company pension funds, the growing incidence of redundancy and early retirement has meant that the leavers are being compensated at the expense of those who stay for the duration. The personal pension allows limitless flexibility for the individual, at little burden for the FD or the company, even if the Chancellor has made it less attractive through ACT. However, when PEPs cease in 1999, a personal pension will almost certainly become the standard method for provision for old age. The government will not be able to meet the pension demands in 2010, so it should think carefully before it disincentivises individuals.

Conclusion

Although this chapter is about the FD as financial manager, the purpose has not been to set out a textbook treatise on financial reporting and accounting. These are tasks for which all qualified accountants are trained and prepared. In such a small space it is more important to stress the need to report in an accurate and timely manner, producing the performance and other financial information required by management and outsiders in a form which shows it clearly and consisely. Financial performance is only one perspective on the overall measure of the organisation's achievement against its strategic objectives. Furthermore, the information given must meet the need at all times and it is the FD's role to ensure it is understood. This includes helping managers, for example, to understand its significance and consequences.

As with other chapters, there has been an attempt to capture a flavour of change. Finance is not and cannot afford to be a static science. Finance is an overhead. It will only be supported for as long as management can see a clear need for the function. As with all other activities in the organisation, it must be possible to see the added value.

Finally, the FD as financial manager will be expected to lead or recommend financial strategy (and funding and financing strategy where the role of treasurer is combined into the FD's responsibilities). In the earlier reported surveys on the future role of FDs, strategic leadership and management accounting were seen as the most important functions of the

FD over the next five years (*see* Chapter 2). The importance of and responsibility for strategic planning and information systems are expected to grow rapidly. The emphasis will continue to move from doing activities to supporting and thinking activities.

As the breadth and importance of the role continues to grow, so will the need for those skills to be totally integrated into, and often possessed, by the whole of the team. The FD will need to use and evolve methods and practices which are more meaningful to the dynamic organisation managing through constant change. This chapter has touched on some of those changes while not invalidating the fundamental need for meaningful reporting and accounting.

This book is intended to set the traditionally accepted role of the FD, i.e. financial and management accounting, in the context of changing organisations in a changing environment and the needs which will thereby arise. The modern FD will understand and anticipate those needs in order to play a full part in the team management of the enterprise. Too often in the past, the FD has acted as a brake on the organisation: controlling and cutting costs; saying what cannot be done, rather than helping to find ways that things can be done; producing out of date information in a form and manner that is incomprehensible, unhelpful or even useless to management. This cannot happen in future.

The FD of course has to ensure that the statutory and fiduciary activities are performed to an expected standard and to help safeguard the probity and viability of the organisation through its agreed governance processes. After that the FD's role is to share in and where appropriate lead the vision and management of the organisation, facilitate information processes and advise, guide and support where appropriate.

The last word is left to David Timson:

> Of course it never was the case that finance directors have been merely bean counters. Financial reporting and control, while important, will increasingly be seen as part of the established culture of successful companies rather than the specific responsibility of an individual. The greater part of the finance director's contribution will be to the future of the business through strategic planning, corporate finance and financial structuring. In these roles, it is hard to avoid the conclusion that an MBA may be an equally valuable qualification as accountancy. (Timson, 1997, Managing Partner, The Curzon Partnership).

7

The FD as accountant

Having said that the modern FD does not need to need to be an accountant, it is important to make clear that this does not mean that the vast majority of FDs will not be accountants for the foreseeable future. Indeed, the profession itself is changing in a number of ways. First, a glance at the columns of the financial press and professional magazines, especially the *Financial Times*, *Accountancy* and *Management Accountant*, shows how the role of the accountant is broadening, let alone that of the FD. Apart from needing to be aware of the developing issues in organisations, either as professional in practice or in industry, the nature of all managerial roles is becoming holistic.

Between them, the aforementioned journals provide a valuable source of technical and practical information, sufficient to alert the FD to the latest financial issues and accounting requirements, both management accounting and financial accounting. Furthermore, they also provide a reference source, either through in-depth articles or briefs, as to what the FD should be aware of and where to find the information.

FDs may not be accountants themselves, but they will be expected to be responsible for the accounting functions of the organisation, except in those few companies which have a separate financial controller. In a SME, the FD, CFO or equivalent will be responsible for accounting and a great deal more. Furthermore, in the latter case, there will almost certainly be more accounting in the role than in a larger organisation, unless the accounting and tax are contracted to a firm of accountants. In this case, there may not be even a CFO, with accountants reporting direct to the owner/proprietor, the MD or the board.

Areas of responsibility

As stated at the outset, this book is not a textbook, especially not an accounting textbook. Having made the case for FDs to be more strategic and concern themselves with the present and the future, this does not in any way obviate the responsibility for historical accounting and reporting and the duty to do so in keeping with all relevant statutes, regulations and best practice. While the FD may not be a member of a CCAB accounting body, the auditors will. The company accounts are required to comply with the Companies Act, Stock Exchange regulations (where relevant), etc. A duty is laid on the directors to comply and, acting as the agent of the shareholders, the auditors are required to report on compliance of the accounts and annual reports.

The duties of the FD will therefore extend to ensuring such compliance, together with the statutory requirement laid on the directors that the accounts will show a true and fair view. Any qualified accountant should also take account of the standard conventions:

going concern; accruals; consistency and prudence; in producing a set of accounts. If the FD employs an accountant to prepare the accounts, whether inside or outside the organisation, they will be bound by this, as will a qualified auditor in reviewing them.

Inter alia, the matters included in this section, where not covered elsewhere, include: accounting and financial control; accounting standards; reporting; regulation and statutory returns; provisions and contingencies; goodwill and intangibles; corporate tax accounting and planning; VAT; cross-border accounting, taxation and transfer-pricing.

Accounting and financial control

The process of accounting itself is not difficult these days. With the power of computing and the availability of packages, all the key processes can be automated. Many software providers have a modularised suite of accounting packages which would include all the key components: general ledger, cash, accounts payable and receivable, ordering and purchasing, invoicing and statements, VAT, etc. Furthermore, all of them will come with much of the functionality not only for financial reporting, but also management accounting and management information.

It is just as important to have distributed accounting and reporting as centralisation. The FD needs to be able to report corporate performance, but managers need real-time information to manage the business proactively in competitive markets. Some financial packages may seem to be sledge hammers to crack a nut but with the power and functionality they carry, they can be much more economical and efficient than growing your own, even if you do not use all the 'bells and whistles'. Having to modify your own management processes in order to match the accounting processes may not be the problem that it is first perceived to be, and any review can produce improvements as a by-product.

Another alternative is to outsource all the accounting. Some very large concerns in the private and public sectors have followed this route and, of course, many SMEs have always operated this way because of the cost of establishing a finance 'factory'. Either way, the benefits may be just as great in terms of better business focus as in economy. The virtual corporations which are now springing up would not dream of creating large, deep traditional functional hierarchies, when they can contract these services elsewhere. What they do need even more, however, are strategic thinking, financial leadership, advice, guidance and support. Whether the FD is an accountant or not, as the role evolves, the breadth of demand and the strain of the rapidly changing business environment will force many to delegate such services outside the organisation, so that a sharper focus can be placed on the areas given greater importance between the covers of this book.

True and fair view

One thing a FD cannot escape from is the need to report the 'true and fair view' in the periodic statements. Varying degrees of skill and competence have led, in the past, to differing practices until standards were established. Where such standards relate to the valuation of assets, the distinction between revenue and accounting transactions, etc., comparative and even absolute statements of financial performance have at times become meaningless. This has been drawn to attention elsewhere, by such as Terry Smith. Unfortunately, I am also of the view that the standards, though well-meaning, have not always helped. Some of them are amazingly complex. Where P/E ratios are calculated having a mind to all such requirements, together with varying industry practices, timing differences, etc., one is left with a measure which can be highly unreliable. Cash based valuations offer a consistent basis for measurement, and are directly related to the company's ability to continue trading, to sustain its credit rating (cash flow is the primary benchmark in the famous CAMEL process), or even to invest in its future. Cash flow accounting and forecasting are therefore essential skills of the FD.

Financial reporting standards (FRSs) and statements of standard accounting practice (SSAPs) and other professional 'advices' have wrestled with the problems of such as: materiality, goodwill, derivatives, research and development, tangible and intangible assets, cash, pensions, future cost, smaller companies, subsidiaries and associates, the PFI, year 2000, insurance, taxation, VAT, depreciation, contingencies, investments and capital, acquisitions and mergers, etc. All of this adds to the complexity, both of the reporting process, and the accounts themselves. While this is necessary to achieve integrity and consistency in the reporting process, very few people outside fund managers and analysts actually read the accounts and by the time they are published, they are months out of date (a year or more with some smaller entities). If there has been any material difficulty, it will probably have been reported as a profit warning earlier. However, I must stress, I am not seeking to undermine the standards and reporting process. I am seeking simplification, especially in respect of the FD's role, in order that they can carry the growing portfolio of demands and concentrate on adding value to the corporation.

Accounting standards and audit practice

As was implied earlier, the FD of a company must take account of these, whether or not they are a qualified accountant, as they are covered by statute through the 1985 Companies Act. All such standards as approved by the Accounting Standards Board are therefore given the force of law through the Act, including especially SSAPs and FRSs. The only reasonable exemption is given for small and medium sized companies (as defined by the Act). Otherwise, all published accounts and reports must be in accordance with the standards and must state where there have been material departures.

As the EC plays a closer role in the management of the UK economy and with the development of global markets, the International Accounting Standards (IAS), will increasingly apply. This will throw up some interesting dichotomies (e.g. on pensions), where the domestic and international standards are not necessarily in harmony. For anyone assuming the reins of FD who needs to recognise and understand what is required of them, the Institute of Chartered Accountants of England & Wales publishes a minutely detailed copy of the latest and complete requirements of ASB (Accounting Standards Board) and indeed the APB (Auditing Practices Board), as do other bodies. *Accountancy* magazine has a technical update section every month, to keep abreast of standards as they are published for discussion, as they are approved and evolve. This book is not the appropriate medium to list or discuss all the relevant standards.

So, while the FD does not need to know the detail of these, he or she does need to know what is required in general terms, where to find the information and, most of all, who is going to make certain of compliance and provide the means whereby the directors can be assured that they have carried out their duties properly, in respect of reporting and accounts and of the consequences where they have not. Usually this will fall to the external auditor, but this does not in any way exonerate the directors from their duties, except where the auditor has misled the directors in some way.

As the incidence of litigation against auditors grows, it is certain that a growing number of companies will be unable to find someone to carry out the statutory audit. Where the FD and the directors are knowingly misleading the shareholders, refusing to comply with their duties, or materially negligent (such as refusing to carry out a year 2000 audit, knowingly or negligently failing to plan for and achieve year 2000 compliance, or in respect of other matters, such as preparing for EMU, or managing derivatives, etc.), an auditor would be absolutely right to resign, publicly stating their reasons for doing so.

The Auditing Practices Board was established in 1991, also by CCAB and, while its remit relates to the auditing activities of any member of the accounting professions who audits any financial statement (including internal auditors), these are of relevance to the FD. The objectives of the APB are to lead the development of auditing practice in the UK and Eire so as to establish high standards of auditing, meet the developing needs of users of financial information and ensure public confidence in the audit process. These will have a direct effect on the duties and responsibilities of the FD, even if the accounting processes are delegated.

The FD will need to be aware, directly or indirectly, of the APB requirements, to the same extent as the ASB and IAS standards, either because the financial statements must accord with the latter, or because they will be audited with regard to the former. Where an audit committee has been established, the auditor should report informally to the FD and management on such compliance and formally to the directors, through the audit committee. Failure to comply with any of this plethora of standards should lead to qualification of the accounts if material, reporting to management or directors if not (depending on significance and whether or not action has been taken).

In the event of major risk to the corporation through such as failure to achieve year 2000 compliance, or even to start the process, this should at least lead to qualification and, where the organisation's viability is at risk, almost certainly resignation by the auditors. If there have not been thousands of such qualifications by late 1998, many auditors will be facing future litigation and some FDs and other directors will be facing personal liability. Survey information shows that a frightening proportion of companies have not taken any steps at all. By early 1998, it was already too late for most of these, (despite Tony Blair's 20 000 'Bug Busters' and almost certainly including parts of government) short of replacing much of their information systems and overhauling their internal processes.

Goodwill, intangibles and brand

The accounting bodies have wrestled with the problem of goodwill for nearly 20 years. I will make an exception to the discussion of Standards in this case only, because the 21st century will be as significant for its exploitation of brand as it will be for any other economic factor. I do not propose to comment on whether the FRS10 is right, wrong, workable or unworkable, other than to say that goodwill could be treated in different ways for different purposes. It is entirely logical, but a little unfortunate that intangibles were included in the same FRS.

So what should the FD be thinking about and how can goodwill arise? The two most obvious situations are in the case of acquisitions and brands. The dictionary definition of goodwill is 'an intangible asset taken into account in assessing the value of an enterprise and reflecting its commercial reputation, customer connections, etc.' (Collins English Dictionary). Brand is defined in the same source as 'a trade name identifying a manufacturer or a product; a trademark'. Here are the complications immediately. From this, the three situations in which goodwill may arise are: on acquisition of a business, during the ordinary course of business, and, by investment of tangible or intangible value in a name or trade mark.

Dealing with acquisition: at the time of purchase, an acquiring company may rationalise that it is paying extra for goodwill, but what it is really paying for is a stream of future earnings. If you buy on a higher P/E ratio than your own, you are potentially diluting your existing earnings. So why do companies do so and as a result create goodwill? The answer lies in the four components which can affect that future stream of earnings:

- The first and most short term is the disruption factor. When two organisations are combined, even as subsidiary and parent, or peer to peer, there will be loss of momentum for both the acquired and acquiring company. As well as the one-off rationalisation costs (such as redundancy), there will be less easily identified opportunity, project and other costs, until the rationalisation process settles down. These have a net present value and could therefore be turned into a future stream of costs over say 20 years (the period over which goodwill might be amortised or written off).

- The second element is the potential cost savings (or economies of scale) which may arise from the combination (I am not sure that these are always realised in net terms).

- The third element is the goodwill acquired, which might comprise 'customer connections' or 'brands'. This might be notionally calculated as the incremental, repeat sales, long-term 'tailoff' value, of those customers and brands, over and above that of a random group of customers producing one-off sales. For example, if a bank bought an insurance company, with loyal customers, what would be the value of additional long term insurance sales that could be made to that customer base?

- The final element is in the ability of the acquiring organisation to cross-sell other products to that customer base, or to transfer the brand values acquired to its own products and customer base.

All of these could be estimated and reduced to a net present value, or turned into incremental revenue streams. Therefore, brand and goodwill may have value and can be investments in just the same way as tangible assets. Given that tangible assets have to be depreciated (including pubs, for example), it would appear prudent to amortise goodwill over, say, 20 years. Brands are created by reputation, which in turn is created either or both by applying cash (through advertising and other marketing), or intangible values (such as customer service or trust), to product or company names. If this investment in the brands is not sustained, the goodwill will decline. Furthermore, brand value or goodwill can be destroyed or damaged very easily and companies do not write goodwill down as a result, despite the obvious effects on future earnings.

This all makes a nonsense of P/E as a measure of the long-term value of a company. While P/E will be reflecting the current stream of earnings of companies and their brands, the value of the latter will be different in different circumstances. All the privatised companies have increased in value dramatically under private ownership. Part of this reflects a transformation in goodwill and the application of different brands. Brand value can be destroyed or damaged overnight, e.g. Hoover, British Gas, etc. The discussion is put forward here for the FD to decide. The debate on goodwill, valuation of brands and intangible assets will continue. My own view is that brand value can be carried indefinitely, but it should at least be written down when disasters occur.

Corporation tax, accounting and planning

As has been explained elsewhere, the potential gains or losses from getting tax right or wrong are so significant, and tax has become so highly specialised, that only the largest companies can afford the resource to optimise tax management. Because of its materiality to the company's fortunes, it must be well-managed. For any company of any size which is involved in transactions overseas, taxation becomes potentially the most complex area to understand and therefore to optimise – even more so than derivatives, because the latter are a common currency all over the world, traded on only a few markets. Tax is different in every single one of the over 200 sovereign states which now exist.

The answer therefore is that the FD should use a tax specialist to get this part right. There is no requirement to pay more tax than you need. The public is not yet concerned about the ethics of corporation tax avoidance, although evasion is of course a crime. If tax laws are complicated, there will always be opportunities for arbitrage. If tax avoidance were outlawed, or even as loopholes are closed, more commercial organisations will become located or domiciled in the most financially attractive countries. Tax, interest rates, cost of labour, grants, inflation and currency factors will be among the major considerations.

Where I have worked in the private sector as a FD or MD, I have always employed an internal tax advisor to manage the process of minimising the tax bill. This did not mean that they did all the work, because where appropriate they worked with external partners for a fee. The most obvious would be the company's auditors. Even in the public sector, we took VAT advice to minimise our bills, because we had no means of recovery without a commercial product to sell. Tax is now highly specialised and complicated. Very few can optimise tax on their own, without access to outside help, especially where overseas tax is involved.

VAT, cross-border, transfer-pricing

What applies to tax is true to a lesser extent of VAT. The growing convergence in Europe will help. Elsewhere in the world, similar arrangements prevail, including purchase tax, sales tax, etc. Even in the UK, VAT is a highly specialised area. When it comes to cross-border considerations on value-added taxes, sales taxes, corporation or any other taxes for that matter, especially double taxation, the FD has more than enough to do, without trying to understand this one area of enormous complexity.

Of course it is the FD's responsibility to give best advice to the board on the company's tax arrangements. The board would expect the FD to lead that process and own the consequences, but this does not obviate the use of external advisors or service providers, as for outsourced accounting services. The key is, who can add greatest value where? There are many areas where the modern FD can add value and, while they should expect to be sufficiently up to date to be able to ask the right questions, there must usually be a net payback from using external advisors in these highly complex areas. This would not be true to the same extent with managing interest rate, currency or balance sheet risk, through, for example derivatives. Here, I would expect the FD (or, where appointed, a treasurer) to take the lead, even if it is to hedge completely the entire risk, for only an executive of the organisation can understand the detail of its own internal objectives and constraints and the complexity of its own cash flows, as well as having the ability to manipulate them where appropriate.

Transfer-pricing will always provoke debate. It is fraught with possibilities for disagreement. One subsidiary's profit can be another's or the group's loss, which when taken as a whole is an illusion. Where overseas operations are involved, the whole process can be highly complex, with limitless opportunities for legitimate manipulation. Once again, a common currency for valuation is cash generation.

Anything which takes costing, absorption and allocation into account can only be fraught with subjectivity. Ideally all accounting would be transparent. Whenever I have been involved with transfer-pricing, it has always led to disagreement on the basis adopted, which can be highly demotivating to the manager who feels he or she is losing out in the equation. The theoretical answer is value-added.

Conclusion

I am clear that while the FD is responsible for the accounting processes, others can usually do this better and cheaper. I am more interested in accounting for the future – management accounting. In this area, the traditional approaches are fraught. Value added is the only rational, consistent basis. In a fast changing world, the value of a brand is totally dependent on the organisation's ability to manage cash flow and to behave appropriately in the customer's or public's eye. Brand and the ability to add value can be destroyed in 24 hours, if the company fails, partially or totally. What value will attach to brand or goodwill, if your organisation cannot account or does not exist on 1 January 2000? Or if you cannot account for and therefore buy or sell goods or services priced in Euros? Or if inadequate, ignorant, incompetent, negligent or criminal management of financial risk leads to the net worth of the company being obliterated by an interest rate change, a currency movement, or the movement of an index?

The challenge for FDs is to know what is happening now and what is likely to happen in the future, what are the likely business and financial consequences, what advice, guidance and support should be given, what are the choices and what is the optimal way forward. They should know instinctively that historical accounting is being properly managed, sufficient to assure the directors and stakeholders that this captures the 'true and fair view' in keeping with whatever standards or conventions are laid down at a point in time. But they must know for sure that the assets are secure, that the balance sheet is being optimised and that there is no reasonable unknown or undue risk which has not been allowed for, taken account of, or managed. Historical accounts are just that – they may have academic meaning for accountants, analysts, fund managers, etc., but the real information is that which assures the ability to generate future revenue streams of value, subject to a managed level of risk.

The FD is responsible for both aspects of accounting, but there is no value in the past, other than what is tied up in the usable, or realisable, value of your assets, especially cash. All other meaningful value in the 21st century lies in an increasingly volatile and unpredictable future. This is the real challenge for accounting and the real opportunity for the FD.

If you do not agree, ask an expert to value your assets on an ongoing basis and a 'fire sale' basis (or a non-year 2000 compliant basis). Where is the real value now, other than in cash and market investments and the people, whose value you do not even capitalise in the balance sheet? Their inherent ability to add value to your business may be immeasurably greater than any goodwill you may attach to your name or processes. How do we account for their knowledge, talent and expertise in a world which has been made insecure through downsizing? Yet their commitment, creativity, flexibility, adaptability and most of all loyalty, could make the difference between success and failure.

8

The FD as treasury manager

Outside the banking and financial services sectors and several large organisations, the treasury function will usually come under the responsibilities of the finance director. Where the treasury function is sufficiently large or important, there will usually be a treasurer reporting to the finance director, otherwise the duties will be combined with the other responsibilities of a member of the finance team, or even carried out by the FD.

Where the FD does not carry the responsibility, there will either be a treasury director or equivalent, or the treasurer will report through another director. Whoever performs the role must have a close working relationship with the finance function in order to ensure proper control and accounting and also to facilitate funding and financial planning. The latter arrangements would also ensure that one of the fundamental principles of treasury management was established, i.e. separation of function. In some large organisations with substantial cash flows, especially where there is a high proportion of foreign currency transactions, treasury will be established as a completely separate division, probably a profit centre in its own right and sometimes a subsidiary company.

In different ways, the FD and the treasurer are responsible for protecting and enhancing shareholder or stakeholder value. In a company, the areas of a treasurer's activities which have a direct bearing on shareholder value include: funding, foreign exchange, interest rate management and liquidity management (including credit risk assessment). For the purposes of this book it is assumed that the FD has responsibility for treasury.

The role of treasury

The treasury role has many aspects which either contribute to protecting or enhancing shareholder value, reducing risk or securing the cashflow of the organisation. Minimising borrowing costs would be a primary function. Managing currency risks would be another. Other key areas are funding and debt management and the investment of surplus funds while ensuring that cash flow is always available when needed. If treasury can make a profit contribution without a material increase in the financial risk profile, then that is a welcome bonus. As recent cases such as the Barings collapse have shown, it is critically important that the board knows what is going on, and that clear controls are established and operating effectively.

The establishment of an asset/liability committee (ALCO) to review policy, controls and the agreed level of risk is highly desirable where the level of risk is potentially substantial. In any case, every board should include at least one non-executive with specific treasury experience and understanding. If the function is under the direction of the FD, then he or she must also have a good working understanding of these complex and potentially risky responsibilities. We now live in a world of global risks where the use of derivatives has exploded. Not only are the latter highly risky, they are also highly complex. In addition, over ninety-five per cent of currency transactions in the London markets are made for speculative rather than trading purposes. Volatility is a fact of life and it takes sound judgement, good experience and a cool nerve to manage treasury in the modern organisation.

Cash management

Every organisation has cash to manage (including banking and borrowing). The FD must ensure the optimum use of cash without undermining its safety and security. There is complexity even in performing this function. For example, any transaction carries inherent risk: e.g. money may not arrive on time, in the right place or at all and the counterparty or an intermediary involved in the transaction may fail and leave the FD having to chase the money, maybe losing interest, unable to complete a transaction dependent on the receipt of that cash, or even suing for the cash on default. A great deal of care and professional judgement needs to go into the systems, processes, receipt, payment and investment of cash.

Planning and managing working capital is a fundamental responsibility of the FD. The treasurer may implement the transactions which obtain cash, e.g. by borrowing, or which ensure that cash is available when needed by planning the maturity of investments, but the FD has an inescapable duty to ensure that working capital is always available to manage the business and to warn of possible problems before they occur. Profit is not cash. True, the difference between the sales and costs of goods produced leads to a cash flow, but there are so many non-cash transactions (such as depreciation) and timing differences (such as late payment) that it is dangerous to look on a profitable organisation as being cash-sufficient. In its simplest form, the production process leads to the raw materials and labour costs being paid before the sales income is received. Furthermore, where sales are in decline and stocks are building up, the period end report can show an over optimistic picture of the actual cash flows. Sales income is accrued for before receipt (debtors) and inventories represent accumulated production costs for goods which may not be sold.

Where a company is operating or transacting outside the UK, even the most basic risks are multiplied. As well as currency risk, there are many other problems, such as different tax regimes and payment systems; less or even harsher regulation; different practices; exchange controls; etc. When all else fails, the best course is to deal with or through well known and reputable institutions, either in the country or through agencies of a UK bank, for example, who know the local conditions. With sound institutions, one has the assurance that funds will arrive unless the counterparty fails or there is for example a systems failure. This does not mean that one should necessarily avoid all other institutions. The greater the risk, the better the price, but caveat emptor prevails. With all risks, taking on extra requires a higher degree of sophistication and knowledge, together with the right balance of supervision and control of the function.

Far too often in the past, the FD or a subordinate has been left with responsibility for investment of surplus cash, with little training or experience. Very many FDs have learned how to manage and make investments on their own, sometimes through their own mistakes. When risk is present, especially in foreign exchange, commodities or more risky investments, there is a great deal at stake (sometimes the viability of the company, as many examples have shown) and a great deal to lose. It is tempting to increase risk in order to try and achieve higher returns, especially where money has been lost on previous transactions. The harsh experience of Barings is the worst example in recent memory. Sadly, there are many more.

The most fundamental rule of treasury is separation of function. The same person must never be responsible for dealing and accounting for transactions. Combining these functions can lead to excessive, uncontrolled speculation being concealed while the dealer tries to recover an extended position, or even to fraud, as more organisations are experiencing. Ultimately it is the responsibility of the board, audit committee or ALCO to know what is going on and what controls exist.

Managing risk, volatility and global markets

It is fair to say that for many businessmen the people who run the international financial markets vie for unpopularity alongside journalists and politicians. The markets are responsible for damaging currency instability, bring pressure on governments to raise base rates when it is not in the country's interest to do so, and force short-termist strategies on managers....Businesses have to learn to live with markets, and use them to their advantage. Derivative markets are all about controlling financial risk, or hedging against unexpected outcomes. Few would deny that international business is easier to transact in an era of liberalised markets and greater global liquidity. That there is occasionally a downside in greater financial turbulence than is warranted has to be accepted as a way of life. (David Smith, Economics Editor of the *Sunday Times*, in *Management Today*, February 1995).

One of the critical considerations for any FD is the organisation's amount of financial exposure. There are sophisticated systems and methods for quantifying this (the global exposure). Very few organisations have the capability or the awareness of their total exposures. In treasury terms, the net exposure on the total sum of financial investments and instruments, currency, commodity contracts, etc. can be calculated. Total exposure goes beyond this, however. Every business decision or transaction has a commensurate set of risks. Where these cannot be precisely calculated, they can be estimated through a 'what if' or scenario process, etc. Once these risks have been identified and evaluated and the financial consequences estimated, the FD can decide what to do about them. This is the process of risk management. Insurance may be bought but this may not cover all the risks and in some cases may be excessive or unnecessary.

Risk management should fall within the FD's responsibilities where there is no separate designated function. Ideally there will be a regular risk audit (perhaps linked to the annual insurance review), a risk manual, designated officers responsible for delegated areas of risk throughout the organisation (comprising the risk team) and a process for evaluating the global risks. Treasury is the most important of the risk functions in an organisation. No organisation is immune. The failure of computer systems or the loss of a significant investment could lead to the failure of the organisation. Lack of cash brings organisations down before lack of capital. On a more mundane level a scientific approach to risk management can not only lead to more informed insurance decisions, but also impresses the insurance company. Both can save money on premiums.

> Most of the disasters which have occurred in the management of financial risk are primarily attributable to the failure of the board fully to understand what was going on in the company's name. And within the board, whose responsibility is it to have the necessary expertise but the finance director? In years gone by, it may have appeared perfectly respectable and reasonable for a finance director to have a broad yet superficial knowledge of the financial markets. The reason the finance director employed a treasurer and a tax manager was to provide the detailed expertise he did not have personally. This is no longer good enough. Perhaps the single most important area of detailed technical expertise which group finance directors will need to have is in the area of financial risk analysis. They will need to know how markets, and the instruments traded in them, operate and have a deep enough knowledge to understand what is being presented to them. This is no longer an area which can be delegated. Nor is it really going to be good enough to say 'if I can't understand it we won't do it'. For the international business, inactivity is in itself a danger. The dangers of not hedging international exposures are almost as great as the risks of inappropriate hedging or speculative action. (David Timson, 1995, The Curzon Partnership).

Derivatives

> Specifically, (the FD) should focus on the risk management aspects of financial management, and the opportunities which modern risk management techniques and products bring, including specifically the use of derivatives. Here again, (the FD) should ensure as far as possible, that non-financial colleagues are as literate as possible in the use of these products. (Daniel Hodson, 1995, Chief Executive, LIFFE).

Derivatives are nothing new, especially futures or options. They can of course be traded, but their prime use for a company should be in managing or minimising financial risk. They have a number of potential advantages over other forms of financial instrument, e.g. they can be more liquid; they are more highly geared; they convey the ability to go short as well as long (and thereby hedge a falling market); they can be more tightly specific for managing risk than say stocks, bonds. They have become much more sophisticated in the last 20 years, especially in moving from currency and commodity to interest rate and market index protection. The world wide liquidity in derivatives has grown to such an extent that they are now driving the cash markets rather than just hedging them. Governments and others are becoming concerned at the effect of speculation on economic stability and the effect of currency fluctuations on economic policy. No international organisation can ignore them.

Accounting for derivatives

The British Bankers' Federation (in consultation with the Irish Bankers' Federation) is approved to issue SORPs on appropriate financial topics. In October 1991, it issued a SORP on *Off Balance Sheet Instruments and Other Commitments and Contingent Liabilities*, recognising the growth in off balance sheet transactions, by banks and related financial institutions. In February 1996, a further SORP was published on derivatives and in late summer 1996, recognising the widespread use of derivatives by companies and other institutions on a world-wide basis, the ASB issued a discussion paper to bridge the gap between the huge volume written on how to use them, with very little on how to account for them. Apart from leaving company accounting open to abuse (despite the fundamental requirement to judge and account for a 'true and fair view'), accounting still represents a lesser risk than the inability or inappropriateness of managing financial risk, even without the use of derivatives.

The ASB's discussion paper dealt with two main areas, disclosure and accounting. Its proposals were:

- first, that the organisation's policies and objectives for financial instruments should be discussed in the operating and financial review;

- second, information about levels of risk should be disclosed in the notes to the accounts;

- third, there should be two other disclosures, i.e. the current value of all instruments compared to their book value, and the effect of using hedge accounting.

This paper signalled a move to current value accounting and the need to report the market risk of financial instruments. It had been all too easy simply to record the face value of such instruments, rather than the underlying value, but the change of emphasis also opened up the question of whether changes in value should be reported to the P&L account or the statement of recognised gains and losses. Whatever the outcome of discussion, in terms of accounting and disclosure, the ASB regarded its immediate proposals as best practice, which would inevitably lead to an exposure draft and an accounting standard. I do not propose to comment on the latter.

The FD's role involves strategy, implementation and best practice in accounting. When it comes to derivatives, you may either take a cautious view (i.e. minimise the risk) or a bold view (i.e. manage and trade the risk), or some point in between. What cannot be avoided by either the FD or the board is the need to understand specific and general financial risk and make decisions accordingly. This goes well beyond derivatives.

Use and control of derivatives

In 1994, The Association of Corporate Treasurers published a brief guide to *Risk Management and Control of Derivatives*, written by Derek Ross, then Chairman of ACT and Partner in charge of Treasury for Touche Ross. In it he wrote:

> As a result of some major losses on derivative transactions both in corporate and financial institution environments, a huge amount of material and many reports have been produced on the subject....The main users are of course corporate treasurers of commercial companies, insurance companies and, where allowed, pension funds. These losses have normally arisen due to failure to implement or operate controls at a very basic level....Although the board of directors has ultimate responsibility for the business, it is uncommon for top executives of non-financial corporations to have an understanding of derivatives risk management sufficient personally to exercise direct control over derivative

operations. This responsibility may be delegated to senior management, but notwithstanding this delegation, the board should at least approve the strategies, policies and procedures to be adopted by the company in its use of derivatives. (ACT, 1994).

To help companies in their understanding of derivatives and their possible uses, ACT published two further booklets: *Derivatives for Directors* (1995) and *Uses of Derivatives* (1997). The latter includes a number of case studies, covering the hedging of overseas payments, inflation, interest rate risk, variations in foreign currency sales, varying cashflows arising from sales, commodity prices, improving investment yields on cash, acquisitions, managing long term debt, etc. This gives an insight into the many variations on the use of these instruments. Richard Cookson said:

The huge growth of derivatives markets and a few well-publicised corporate disasters involving these instruments has worried many companies who have contemplated using them....In fact the vast majority of derivatives are not in any sense complex. Many of the instruments which are routinely described as leveraged and dangerous are simple forward contracts. And the problem with tarring all these instruments with the same brush is that it militates against sensible discussion of the very different properties of, say, forward and option contracts, and the way in which these products should be used. Worse, it creates the impression that companies can afford to ignore the financial risks which they run. They can't. (ACT, 1995).

Managing financial risk

To hedge a risk using derivatives is to manage it. Not to hedge it, is to ignore it. The questions are:

* do you understand the financial risks which face the enterprise; can you evaluate these;

* are you consciously managing them (whether by using derivatives or 'natural' methods);

* do you have a strategy, policies and procedures, agreed at board level and understood by all;

* and whether or not you are using derivatives, are you properly accounting for your financial risks?

It is no exaggeration to say that many companies all over the world have failed through the use of derivatives, but how many more have suffered severe setbacks in corporate profits or a savaging of their share price, as a result of failing to understand or manage their financial risks? Derivatives are made out to be highly complex and it is true that understanding some of the more esoteric varieties and combinations requires a degree in maths. The accepted market models (especially Black-Scholes) are robust and mature, so what matters more to the FD is how they match or minimise known risks. These risks, if ignored, can cause major fluctuations in company profitability, making it difficult for the FD to advise management reliably on future performance. Furthermore, where they involve commodity prices or exchange rates, they could have a material impact on pricing decisions. The process starts, therefore, with a basic understanding of the financial risks which corporations face.

Before the 1970s, interest rates were relatively much more stable than in the 1980s and 1990s, and currencies were also relatively stable, based on a system of fixed parities, revised only occasionally. Volatility became an accepted fact of life after the two major oil crises of the 1970s, which led to almost unprecedented levels of inflation in the Western economies (leaving out isolated instances such as the Weimar Republic in Germany). Leaving aside the special types of risk inherent in a treasury operation itself, together with those arising from lack of adequate internal controls, there are several categories of financial risk, most of which can be hedged using derivatives.

Credit risk relates to the risk that individual counterparties to a transaction, or other creditors will fail to meet their obligations. Country risk relates to the possibility that counterparties or creditors in other countries may be unable to fulfil their obligations in part or whole, due to circumstances relating to the political or economic circumstances of that country. It is not unusual to find a country which puts an embargo on exchange of its currency or transmission of funds to other countries, especially where it is in a currency or economic crisis. Finally, there is a whole area of market risks which can arise: interest rate risk, maturity mis-match risk, liquidity risk, open position risk, transaction risk, and currency risk.

What are derivatives?

All these risks, or variants, existed well before the advent of a mature market for derivatives. A derivative is a financial instrument which derives its value from an underlying price or rate. There are essentially three main types of derivative: forward contracts, options, and swaps.

Forwards have been around for centuries. If you bought wool for shipment from Australia, in the days when it took weeks for it to be shipped to the UK, you could deal at a price for future delivery. The difference between a cash price and a forward price has a large element of the interest cost of money and an element of risk.

An option contract gives you the option to buy, or sell, a commodity or amount of money at a given price, at some time in the future (usually up to a given date).

A swap enables you to exchange either a stream of payments in one currency, for a stream in another currency (so changing the currency risk, e.g. from dollars to sterling), and/or a stream of fixed interest rate payments for a stream of variable interest rate payments (giving you the opportunity to change the basis of payments on a debt for example).

All other derivatives are derived from these basic instruments, or combinations of them (e.g. a swaption is a combination of a swap contract and an option contract).

Balance sheet management

This book is not the right place to enter into a treatise on how to use derivatives. The circumstances in which they may be used are relevant to the role of the FD, however. Every balance sheet will probably contain some assets or liabilities which are fixed rate by nature and some which are variable. For as long as there are mismatches in such a balance sheet, the company will be exposed to gains or losses, depending on whether interest rates are going up or down.

There are a number of ways to neutralise these risks, which do not necessarily need to involve derivatives. Firstly, by examining the balance sheet, asset by asset, each asset could be matched with a corresponding liability, on the basis of interest rate (fixed or floating) and duration (an approximation to term). FDs have traditionally preferred fixed rates to variable, to give a high degree of certainty for future commitments. In the case of long term assets, such as property, etc., these could be deemed to be matched by equity. If any reasonable portion of the balance sheet is left deliberately unmatched, the FD is by definition speculating on future moves in interest rates.

Two major factors are causing a swing from equity to debt. The trend to EVA as a measure of corporate performance and the relatively low level of interest rates historically, together with the decline in acquisitions (and corresponding increase in disaggregation) have led to repayment of equity and proportionally higher levels of debt. Indeed, if Stern Stuart had their way, the old benchmark of 1:1 debt to equity might be more like 2:1 or more. Debt is also easier to hedge, because of the ready availability of interest rate based derivatives contracts, compared to equity based. (The latter are primarily in the form of futures on exchange quoted major company shares.)

The three main approaches to financial risk are therefore:

- to do nothing (which is, by definition, speculating on interest rate, inflationary or exchange rate movements);
- to match out all the risks using derivatives;
- or to overmatch or speculate using derivatives, based on the underlying assets or liabilities (sometimes going beyond this and speculating in traded contracts, including by setting up a trading operation).

Foreign exchange and commodities

Foreign exchange and commodities are a necessary evil for a multitude of organisations. Some, such as public sector organisations, should have no exposure to either because of the domestic nature of their transactions. Others, such as building societies, are specifically prohibited from having an exposure to currency risk and do not deal in commodities. Despite this, there are far more risks than might be appreciated, e.g. if the purchase of a major piece of equipment, such as a scanner for a hospital, was made from an overseas supplier, the volatility of a currency could have a material effect on the price. The timing of the purchase could result in variation in price as a result of currency fluctuations, e.g. the price in Deutschmarks could have fallen by twenty per cent or more, during 1997/8.

Many organisations have lost enormous amounts of money and put their viability at risk by speculating in currency or commodity markets beyond their normal commercial requirements. The FD must be aware of such transactions whether or not he or she has accountability for the decisions. Otherwise, there may not be a process for making the board aware of the consequences. Controls, systems and processes must be in place to safeguard the organisation, but if the systems to report the fluctuation of risk even within one working day are either not present, not used, ignored or circumvented, no board would be able to act in time.

EMU

Derivatives are changing and evolving, especially where they are derived from currency transactions. LIFFE was the second futures exchange in the world (after Chicago) and is now at the heart of the UK and European Derivatives markets. It has become the second most important exchange in the world also. As a result, in the UK, you can hedge almost any financial risk. Whilst a hedge is essentially a bet, it has the advantage that it can often be unwound or matched. The best way to look at derivatives is as a means to manage financial risks. Once you look at them as speculative, you are moving into the arena of trading. This is unlikely to coincide with the aims and objects of your business.

So what relevance does this have to EMU? A number of factors are key. First, LIFFE is now under serious challenge. Why? Because of EMU and real-time trading systems. We shall deal with only the former. In 1999, eleven or more European currencies will be replaced by one super-currency – the Euro. Among the most traded foreign exchange contracts after the dollar and sterling are the Deutschmark and the French franc. The epicentre of the Euro will be Frankfurt, which threatens to overtake LIFFE as number two in the world. One of the reasons is that we have eschewed EMU, following the earlier painful experience and because of worries about loss of sovereignty.

I will not argue in favour of or against the Euro and currency convergence. What I will say is that not being in at the start has a number of serious disadvantages for UK FDs.

First, sterling was driven up, partly due to the uncertainty before the Euro. When the Euro settles down, it could slump just as quickly, especially if interest rates are declining. This could coincide with the run-up to 2000 with all the attendant dangers and panic. That is why the UK must be ahead of its trading partners before the crisis happens. This would minimise the consequences, but also maximise the huge opportunities which may exist after the crisis subsides. So any company selling abroad suffered badly in 1997/8 from sterling's strength.

Second, we shall lose out on trading opportunities, not only within the Euro bloc, due to the added costs and complications of currency exchange, but also outside as other trading nations choose to trade with a group of eleven countries where pricing is common.

Third, we have been lulled into an utterly false sense of security because we may not join for at least five years. The consequence is that, where few have prepared fully for year 2000, even fewer have prepared for the Euro. How are they going to buy or sell in Euros if they cannot price or account in the second biggest currency in the world?

Finally, the costs of conversion will be immeasurably greater than if we had gone in in one big bang.

The UK has outperformed the whole of Europe, economically, in the last few years, but, year 2000 aside, is unlikely to do so in the early 21st century. First, the eleven have been held back by the need to meet the entry standards of the Euro, including very high unemployment rates; second, once the Euro settles down, the release of potential energy and the effective favoured status which will exist between the countries within the bloc could see a real growth in trade which would not otherwise have happened. Let us hope we will not be left on the sidelines.

So what is happening in UK companies and what should concern the FD? As with year 2000, there will be a number of camps:

- Some do not see the problem at all, especially if they do not do business in other currencies. What they fail to realise is that opportunities may open up through being able to transact in Euros and that there will be indirect consequences which could change patterns of trade and flows of goods and resources – including labour!

- The next group will see the threat but feel unable or unwilling to do anything about it. With any transactions in the relevant currencies, they could see wild swings or dramatic loss of business or sources of supply.

- The third group may have planned or effected the necessary changes as a damage limitation exercise.

- The final group will see a potentially limitless opportunity. They recognise that any such dramatic change produces opportunities for trade arbitrages and will plan to capitalise accordingly. Part of their gain will be made at the expense of their UK based competitors. The UK economy may suffer, if the balance of trade swings adversely.

By now it will be clear that the Euro is a *fait accompli*. Most of the challenges for the FD have already been covered by implication. The two most significant will be the changes to systems which will be unavoidable for many companies; and the change of attitude, which will minimise risk and create opportunity. Ironically, Britain would have been as well placed as any country, both economically and on the Maastricht criteria, to join. It seems beyond doubt that we would have capitalised at others' expense. Some of the larger multinationals may still do so. In the meantime, the first British Euro account was opened by Natwest for Siemens in March 1998.

Funding and financing

One of the treasury functions of the FD is ensuring the availability of short and longer term finance. The former will usually be for the purposes of cash flow management. The latter may be for planning longer term cash flow but will more often be related to investment in capital projects, acquisitions, etc. For the company, both equity and debt are available. For other organisations, only borrowing is applicable.

Matching is a key technique for all funding and financing. The FD will try to match the pattern of cash flows, to iron out peaks and troughs and also for longer term funding may seek to match the duration of liabilities to that of the underlying asset which is to be funded. This latter is critical to financial institutions whose balance sheets are almost exclusively comprised of cash assets and liabilities, financial instruments and commitments and funding instruments. For the company, fixed assets with a long life span will often be matched by finance of a similar duration, e.g. long term debt or equity. The FD will often find fixed rate finance preferable for funding such assets.

When equity is available, the question of gearing comes into play. This is also where earlier comments about not ignoring financial risk are pertinent. To ignore a financial risk is the same as to take one. Each leaves an unmatched exposure to volatility in markets and economic circumstances which can lead to an unplanned loss of value. This is where matching assets and liabilities or the use of derivatives are relevant. Whether or not the FD has responsibility for the treasury function, the need to be aware of and quantify specific and net financial risks to profit cannot be avoided by the FD.

This report does not allow for a long treatise on the enormous range of funding instruments, issued in a growing number of world markets, all of which are linked by global factors. Careful selection can not only reduce the cost but also the risk of funding by, for example, spreading it. There are risks to borrowing as well as lending. The counterparty might fail. Interest rates or currencies may move against your expectations. The risks and the opportunities need to be understood by the FD. Treasury and risk management will increasingly be functions of the FD of the future.

Debt management, funding and finance are interlinked with the overall management of working capital. While minimising debtors and fairly stretching creditors can improve working capital dramatically and thereby save on borrowing costs or release funds for investment, planned management of cash flows can also produce efficiency savings in interest terms. The FD should always have ready access to cash flow projections, whether or not he or she is responsible for the funding of shortfalls or the investment of spare cash.

Where there is a long term surplus of cash, the investment term or liquidity and thereby the return on an investment can be stretched, based on objective analysis and considered judgement. (Resorting to external advice may help, but the ultimate decision must always be that of the FD or treasurer. Abdication of responsibility for the decision to an external party does not exclude responsibility for the consequences.) Where there is a long term shortage or funds are needed for a specific project, such as a capital investment or acquisition, etc. financing comes into play. Here the FD will need to consider the whole of the balance sheet and the duration of each asset or liability.

Help is at hand

The demands on the FD will continue to grow. Many more specialist functions could be added to the portfolio. It is no surprise in the field of treasury, that more members of the Association of Corporate Treasurers are being recruited to the FD's office and more existing FDs are seeking to join the Association. For those who are neither, the Association and its regular publications and courses are an excellent source of information and guidance (including *The Treasurer* magazine). The *Treasurer's Handbook* carries a particularly good section on good practice guidance in a number of areas such as foreign exchange and money market dealing procedures, tax treatment, accounting standards, treasury policies and dealing mandates, fraud and money laundering, etc.

Many FDs will need to become aware of the requirements of the City Code of Conduct and the Financial Services Act, which regulates investment business carried on by a corporate treasury and, together with the Stock Exchange listing requirements and other regulations, have a direct bearing on listed securities in the UK. Matters become even more complex overseas. For example, to issue in Japan you will need the Ministry of Finance approval and a rating from an accepted credit rating agency.

Conclusion

As for the FD as an accountant and a professional (see Chapter 17), integrity, ethics and sound professional conduct are fundamental to the treasury role. High standards are both laid down and expected in the UK, which has taken a lead in world markets. 'My word is my bond' is good enough to seal millions of transactions every day, but it is the detailed systems, procedures and controls in the markets and individual organisations which make it all work. Treasury is not a function to be taken lightly by any organisation. Not only can bad management damage your wealth, but it can also damage your reputation, goodwill and corporate brand in increasingly competitive markets.

Whether as manager responsible for treasury, control and accounting, quantification of risk, audit or governance, the board should have a right to rely on the competence, awareness and professional judgement of its finance director. Treasury and risk management are not spare time occupations or pleasant diversions. They are fundamental to the viability of the organisation.

9

The FD as auditor; corporate governance

> The need for an effective board has been stressed by every student of the publicly owned corporation in the last 40 years. To run a business enterprise, especially a large and complex enterprise, management needs considerable power. But power without accountability always becomes flabby or tyrannical and usually both. Surely, we know how to make boards effective as an organ of corporate governance. Having better people is not the key; ordinary people will do. Making a board effective requires spelling out its work, setting objectives for its performance and contribution, and regularly appraising the board's performance against these objectives. (Drucker, 1992).

For a quoted company, if its board is not working, the verdict is increasingly being given not only by the shareholders and the market, but also by the public. If governance of organisations had been working satisfactorily, there should have been no need for Cadbury. Organisations ought to be expert at regulating and governing themselves. Self-regulation has also been shown not to work in the City and the financial services markets (e.g. mis-selling of pensions and the Barings collapse).

We have had Cadbury, Greenbury and now the Hampel committee has reported. The public outcry against the mismatch between inflated corporate salaries and corporate performance has been picked up by political parties and some fund managers (who are now the biggest holders of quoted shares), or trustees of pension funds. All of these themes will be addressed as we review the broader scope and importance of governance, a function which is the responsibility of the board, supported from executive management by the chief executive and the FD. Audit is but one part of that process, increasingly converging with risk management.

The role of the audit committee

Every organisation should have one. While many would see the audit committee performing essentially financial and audit tasks, it can go beyond and provide an excellent means to lighten the load of the board, strengthen the contribution of the non-executive directors and the partnership between the board, management and the auditors. Clearly it is important for adding value to both the internal and external audit processes. External auditors are independent of course, but the audit committee gives an environment for real dialogue and non-confrontational treatment of contentious issues.

The FD often has responsibility for internal audit these days, although many think there should be an independent reporting line. The best way to establish independence of the function is to guarantee a line to the chairman of the board or audit committee if needed and to provide through the committee the same open environment as for the external auditor. The FD while attending the committee would not normally be a member. As with other committees of the board, ideally they are made up solely of non-executive directors (the remuneration committee would be another.) Since Barings and other failures, it will become an increasing practice for the risk manager to work closely with internal audit and have access to the audit committee. This should be complemented by a NED with specific understanding of treasury, especially to lead on matters of financial and balance sheet risk.

While the annual report and accounts should not be the sole focus of the committee, they can consume enormous amounts of time in finalising them before presentation to the board and members for approval. The committee can take on much of this burden and here the FD would lead the process. Equally, if there has been fraud or misappropriation, except in those circumstances where the police need to be brought in immediately, the committee can advise and question management on the facts, satisfying the board of the level of threat to the corporation along the way. Again, the FD, working with both auditors as appropriate, is best placed to lead the initial processes of investigating the loss and determining possible courses of action. Many such losses will of course be dealt with through the FD's office, but it is for the FD to decide on when more serious steps or a higher involvement are merited. I shall return to the matter of fraud.

Governance is very close to the core responsibilities of the audit committee. It cannot usurp the responsibility of the full board but can take much of the weight and, constituted with suitable members, provide leadership and advice as necessary. These committees have become very much more widespread in recent years, in both the private and public sectors. Cadbury recommended that all listed companies which have not already done so should establish an audit committee and placed great emphasis on the importance of properly constituted audit committees in raising standards of corporate governance. *Inter alia* such committees could 'help the finance director, by providing a forum in which he can raise issues of concern, and which he might use to get things done which might otherwise be difficult.'

Cadbury

The Cadbury Committee was set up in May 1991 to report on the financial aspects of corporate governance. Its sponsors were concerned at the perceived low level of confidence both in financial reporting and in the ability of auditors to provide the safeguards which the users of company reports sought and expected. Since then, its recommendations have been reviewed for many other organisations in both the private and public sectors.

That it should have been necessary at all is a sad indictment of directors, regulators and the relevant professions for failures and inadequacies of the past. This is not to say that there were widespread problems, but no-one would deny that in the previous climate, directors, auditors and managers sometimes found themselves in a position where they were either ignorant of, or unwilling parties to, the misstatement of financial reports or inadequate, or non-existent financial controls.

Several well publicised failures before and since Cadbury have confirmed the long overdue need for recommended practice. Corporate governance is the system by which organisations are directed and controlled, from strategy to implementation. Boards of directors or equivalent bodies are responsible for the governance of organisations. While Cadbury looked at the specific financial aspects of corporate governance (i.e. the way in which financial policy is set and overseen, the use of financial controls and the process for reporting on activities and progress of the organisation), its application has spread or influenced corporate activity beyond finance and companies into other areas and sectors of organisation management and direction. It could fairly be claimed that Cadbury marked the formal birth of the profession of corporate governance.

The specific relevance of Cadbury was to directors (especially but not only non-executive directors), finance directors and managers, internal and external auditors. Many boards had become dominated by executive members, inhibiting objectivity and potentially intimidating the non-executive. By no means all boards included a finance director or equivalent. Audit committees did not always exist, especially outside the corporate sector.

The question is, how much change did Cadbury make and will there need to be further changes? Certainly, the public sector (e.g. NHS Trusts), financial services (e.g. building societies) and the private sector have absorbed Cadbury recommendations in the way their boards are constituted and their policy, together with how they report.

> However, 'plenty of senior executives, fund managers and analysts will tell you privately that Sir Adrian Cadbury's Code of Practice on corporate governance is irrelevant and ineffective. A few will say it publicly too.' (Rupert Morris, 1995, *Management Today*).

In my view, it is a failure of governance that any of this is necessary. Any professionally qualified accountant knows instinctively or by training what is right. Furthermore, if auditors are doing their job properly, they are an important adjunct to the governance process. This would be more so if more companies allowed or encouraged a business audit by their auditors.

> It may not be too fanciful to expect that in ten years a major pension fund will not invest in a company's shares or fixed income securities unless that company submits itself to a business audit by an outside professional firm. (Drucker, 1992).

It is true that if there were widespread self-regulation there would have been no need for Cadbury, but too few organisations follow this course. Sadly, the self-regulatory organisation ends up paying for regulation it does not need, and the misdemeanours of its less disciplined brethren. I would only add that the 'good' organisation in this scenario tends to manage better in general, to the benefit of the corporate performance. The good FD will take the lead in governance, working with the board and MD.

A wider role for the board

An interesting development, which showed the wider public interest in governance, was the 1995 publication of the RSA report on *Tomorrow's Company*. This also embraced the concept of the stakeholder, to include shareholders, customers and employees (and by implication the public). The RSA saw the need for individual companies to tailor their responses to new and changing competitive circumstances, together with the 'profound' economic and social changes they face. This model very much coincides with the line taken in this book and its vision of the broader role of the FD of the future.

> Recent changes in accounting standards and corporate governance – partly linked to the Cadbury Report – are re-emphasising the finance director's status as watchdog and corporate policeman. Non-executive directors, newly conscious of their monitoring duties and more visible to the outside world, look to the finance director for technical guidance. (Owen, 1995).

The continuing debate on governance has led some to call for two-tier boards as in Germany and elsewhere. This is a line that the Labour government might take. The point is that if 'unitary' boards perform their function satisfactorily, there should be no need for a senior tier. The role of the executive directors is key to this approach remaining. Non-executive and executive directors can work in partnership for the long term good of the organisation. Each can make a contribution, the aim being improved understanding by the non-executive directors so that they can perform their role on behalf of the stakeholders. The FD's role will be key to providing the relevant information and facilitating the governance process.

> Despite the small number of high-profile collapses, I believe that the unitary Board has served us very well in the UK and that active, independent non-executives should be able to play a more effective role and provide a greater contribution as members of unitary boards. However, the openness and quality of executive directors are and will remain the key factors in ensuring sound corporate governance, enabling non-executives to properly fulfill their roles. (Clive Reay, 1994, BDO Binder Hamlyn).

Assurance

Despite the mixed press it received, several of Cadbury's recommendations have become embedded in best practice. Directors of listed companies were required to report publicly on the effectiveness of the company's system of internal control. Again, I am concerned that what should be common sense has come down to a set of rules, but many organisations have moved forward significantly. The role of the external auditor should not be underestimated. FDs could choose to take a cavalier attitude to such recommendations, but best practice is often set by peer pressure and the highest professional auditing standards. Once the findings of Cadbury and the consequences of such as Barings have been digested, it was easy to see that the processes of assurance and protecting shareholder or even stakeholder interest (including the public at large) might lead to auditors seeking Cadbury type practices and statements to reaffirm their audit judgement.

The Audit Practices Board took these matters on, indirectly supported by the growing tendency to sue auditors when things go wrong. Among the most meaningful concepts which were highlighted are effectiveness, materiality, 'reasonable assurance' and 'reportable weakness'. Matters which can lead to qualification of accounts, or at least be reported to the audit committee, have often been the subject of fierce debate between management and auditors, especially the FD. Where the latter is a member of the top team, responsible for the accounts and the internal audit function, it can feel like a personal affront if there is challenge in some of these areas. Reasonable assurance should be two way for the basis of a constructive relationship between the auditor and the FD, and between both and the board, via the audit committee.

The FD will be working to the highest professional standards, of course. He or she is also concerned to minimise the audit fee and get value for money. The auditor, meanwhile, has statutory, fiduciary and professional duties, not to mention the risk of a lawsuit. Yet there is much in Cadbury and the realm of corporate governance on which a partnership can be based; particularly the possibility of the board, FD, internal auditor, external auditor and even the risk manager working in harmony to deliver real, measurable value in terms of the continuous growth, development and improvement of the organisation's management and business processes. The dividends here, in financial terms, could dwarf any fee. This is especially true for SMEs, through the availability of a welter of professional skills such as treasury.

We shall consider the effectiveness of internal controls in a later section. The latter can be balanced to provide reasonable assurance about accuracy and materiality of the possibility of losses or fraud when taken in conjunction with the evaluation and management of risk. As for effectiveness, if the management team has a concern, it need look no further than the areas identified for improvement of the processes, to find a return on the audit fee. If it is reluctant to accept the unpalatable truth which a 'true and fair view' set of accounts shows, then this defeats the objectivity of governance anyhow.

Year 2000 and viability

While it is regrettable that such advice was needed, what Cadbury said was sound. Indeed, despite the early grumblings captured above, there has been measurable progress, mitigated only by a not unreasonable growing preoccupation by auditors with the problems of unlimited liability. Cadbury raised the subject of 'reportable weakness' and it would be reasonable to assume that an unqualified audit report implied either that there was none, or that management had acted on advice to eliminate the problems. It will be interesting to see whether there is a proliferation of 'year 2000' qualifications in the next reporting year, as many organisations have still made little or no progress in this respect.

In a similar vein, will auditors qualify companies which cannot demonstrate adequacy in managing balance sheet, interest rate or currency risk (let alone the use of derivatives), or even the ability to account in Euros, where they have business with member countries? It may seem to be a matter of degree, but shareholders and stakeholders alike are entitled to know where there is the risk of material loss or failure, before they suffer financial disadvantage themselves from the consequences. This would extend as far as customers who can no longer have their products serviced or replaced because of the failure of the supplier due to a foreseeable problem, especially 'year 2000' compliance.

The Companies Act requires directors to maintain accounting records 'sufficient to show and explain the company's transactions and disclose with reasonable accuracy, at any time, the financial position of the company'. Auditors are required 'to form an opinion as to whether proper accounting records have been kept' and to tell shareholders where this is not the case. Similar requirements are now built in to the regulation of all public bodies. Cadbury was right to take these requirements forward more specifically and reasonably, in the wake of spectacular or even routine failures to do so.

Hampel

Some have said the Hampel report turns the clock back on some of the Cadbury recommendations. It would be most unfortunate if some organisations decided to stop doing and reporting things which are in the public interest. No-one is asking FDs to waste money, and who would be an external auditor these days, when you set the return in a highly competitive market against the litigation risks? We shall shortly see audits that no-one bids for, for exactly that reason. It only needs the threat of disqualification to be made to bite (thousands of active directors have been involved in several failed companies) for unscrupulous practices to go into decline. For as long as any FD or MD sets out to mislead shareholders or others for material gain, we shall need to be told what we must do and how we must report. It is for the very best to set the standard and encourage other FDs and their regulators to act. In the meantime, we will continue to see committees and professional bodies spelling out what we should already know.

So let us look at this objectively. The process of governance should be about setting and delivering a clear, successful strategy. Any objective contributions from auditors, risk managers and directors should be seen as delivering positive value in increasingly competitive environments. The continuous cycle of improvement in processes, in a total quality environment, can only enhance such value. The auditing process should be a partnership, not adversorial. So where does Hampel take us?

First, the paucity of coverage was an interesting comment in itself. There was no headline news like Cadbury. The world has already moved on, either to absorb sound recommendations on best practice, or to avoid or manage the consequences of not doing so. The terms of reference of Hampel's committee were designed to wrap up and consolidate previous formal reviews of corporate governance, especially Cadbury and Greenbury. The five key areas surveyed were:

- the Cadbury Code;
- the role of executive and non-executive directors;
- matters arising from the Greenbury study on directors' remuneration;
- the role of shareholders in corporate governance issues;
- the role of auditors in corporate governance issues.

In addition, the committee had a remit to deal with any other issues relevant to corporate governance in the UK.

It is easy to forget that we are now more than five years after Cadbury, and despite a somewhat mechanistic, formal approach, the tangible changes have been significant. Hampel appeared to turn the clock back in some respects. Of course, making reporting requirements more arduous could be an irrelevance if it is no longer possible to understand a company's accounts, either absolutely or relatively. Furthermore, it can only be a matter of time before 'real-time' reporting becomes standard practice in leading edge organisations, first internally, then externally.

The general tenor of the report is to advocate simplification and ease reporting requirements. The question is whether FDs will use this as an excuse to turn the clock back to pre-Cadbury. All FDs are capable of recognising and producing the true and fair view. If anyone sets out to deceive or mislead, they may get away with it for the time being. If the company fails, the shareholders may even manage to sue the luckless auditor, until the inevitable limited liability and corporate status arrive. Until the corporate world accepts the principle of stakeholder responsibility, private companies will continue to be run for the benefit of their directors.

Responses to Hampel

Now I am not suggesting that more than a few FDs have produced litigiously false accounts. I am saying that in the complexities of accounting standards and the occasional contradictions of accounting, it is possible to put a gloss on corporate or even public sector performance. While rules and regulations may be arduous, they have produced progress, greater objectivity and greater consistency in the last five years. As a former FD, I totally agree with Hampel's recommendation to move towards a more 'principle-based' approach to corporate governance, but I also ask what message it gives to boards and FDs.

Among other matters concluded by Hampel: audit firms were asked to look again at reducing the 10% dependency limit; they should no longer be required to confirm that a company's internal controls are 'effective' but should discuss the matter privately with the directors; the current single statement can be taken to imply an absolute assurance against misstatement or loss. It did not take long for the ICAEW's corporate governance group to call for Hampel to end the confusion in the business community between its proposed statement of principles and the existing Cadbury and Greenbury codes. Going further, Arthur Andersen and its legal arm, Garretts, called for guidance on defining the independence of NEDs. Finally, the ACCA called for the committee to 'ensure the strength, clarity and transparency of the system it proposes', voicing concerns that Hampel could reverse Cadbury gains. Oh dear!

The competent, broad, objective, forward thinking, adaptable FD described between these covers should have little difficulty. Produce a set of accounts which shows a true and fair view in terms of the standards and reporting requirements. Make yourself aware of the risks and deficiencies in management and business processes, as identified through an objective audit process. Define, determine and evaluate the financial consequences of all of these and discuss them with management and the audit committee. Do not be prescriptive or intransigent, but by all means be objectively principled. The organisation exists for all its stakeholders, because if it fails, they all lose, financially and materially.

The FD's role is to facilitate the strategic plan and to ensure understanding of the consequences of management decisions, not to stop them. Having done so, the FD has a duty to report accurately to all interested parties. Prescription by Cadbury, the APB, the ICAEW, or anyone, does not prevent working from first principles and designing the information to be as fast, accurate and helpful as possible to its users. Take the lead and use cash-based and risk-based reporting to augment statutory and regulatory requirements. What matters is for everyone to take a genuine interest in what is really happening. If you achieve this, you will get plaudits from me, Hampel and Cadbury. If your fellow directors disagree, plough another furrow!

Internal control

This book suggests that the role of the FD has become much wider and more complex. The last passage indicates just one of many new factors which the FD needs to take into account. More fundamental to the role is the matter of internal control. In an article in *Accountancy* in May 1995, Peter Carty reviewed the debate and consequences related to internal controls arising out of the Barings disaster.

Nick Leeson was very skilled in using derivatives. He made a lot of money for his employers. Success breeds success. I do not know what controls were in place at Barings, but either they failed (for example by failing to separate dealing from accounting), or they were overridden at dealer level or higher, or they were inadequate. Whatever the truth, controls need to be in place in all the key financial operations of an organisation. They should also include separation of function wherever possible, they should be regularly inspected and reviewed and all the processes subject to regular audit. Ultimately it is the board's responsibility. Much of it is the FD's responsibility to lead, direct, facilitate or advise.

Returning to the subject of directors' and auditors' responsibilities for reporting on internal control, the Auditing Practices Board took up the debate, starting with the publication of a discussion paper *Internal Financial Control Effectiveness*. The good, far-sighted FD will take this subject on as a personal responsibility, consult with auditors and directors and advise the board accordingly. If the review is thorough and adaptable for evolving circumstances, no external body should be able to set higher standards. The organisation's own standards will meet the test when the time comes. This is the essence of good governance – knowledge of the company, understanding of external factors, listening to all views, applying best professional judgement, setting the standard and knowing instinctively it will meet the mark. This is the essence of self-regulation. If every organisation worked proactively in this way, rather than reacting to circumstances, imposed regulation would be less onerous and less costly.

Risk and control self assessment

Returning to the topic of mechanistic approaches to self-regulation, some have advocated the approach called control self-assessment (CSA). The move towards this in the last couple of years appears to have been driven by the desire of central management to regain responsibility for control systems, a move towards continuous improvement as an approach to operations management, better management of risk, demonstration of a tangible process to support Cadbury type requirements on the effectiveness of controls, and fashion. I am not against CSA, indeed I am in favour of anything which concentrates management's thinking on the necessity and implementation of adequate controls, the importance of risk review and management and the whole principle of process improvement. It does seem as though the whole area of corporate governance has been falling back into traditional, left-brain thinking.

In an ideal world, the business will be driven *inter alia* by excellence and flexibility of management and business processes. Appropriate controls, which protect the business without slowing it down, should be built in from the outset. There is no substitute for thinking about what is being done at every stage of the processes and how to improve constantly. An understanding and assessment of risks should be second nature and the consequences of management decisions, including alternative courses, should be available on a real time basis. It is not unreasonable to expect all business managers to be numerate enough to understand this information. FDs can nevertheless facilitate holistic, meaningful understanding of business performance. If controls have to be built in to business processes and systems to avoid obvious risks such as duality of function or fraud, so be it. We are all subject to human frailty to various degrees. If those controls become mechanical or excessive, we have lost the plot.

So where does CSA fit in? It is a formal process where line management takes responsibility for operational controls. The most sophisticated examples effectively formalise the process of continuous improvement, without eliminating empowerment or originality of thought. Once management starts to regard it as routine, there is a risk that a CSA approach may become self-defeating.

CSA is very much a management tool. It has been said that internal and external auditors are the experts in such controls, but if management accepts that, the process is in danger of becoming passive. Like the FD, auditors should facilitate good control and risk awareness. If they are seen to be responsible for implementation or even retrospective reporting, management could lose vigilance, certain that someone else will pick up what slips through the net – maybe too late.

Of course, external auditors have a duty to make sure the owners' interests are secured, but in a modern world, especially the internal auditor should be seen as a consultant working to help management improve the efficiency of processes. It is inevitable that audit and risk management will converge and this element of Hampel is to be welcomed. Despite what has been said above, reliance on active internal control awareness and management will increase as part of a process focused culture, because as we move closer to 'real time' reporting, the responsibility for performance and stewardship of assets will move away from the FD and towards the managers who are accountable for delivery of the corporate plan. If they do not accept this responsibility, they have no right to complain if they perceive the FD as holding up progress or making the scoring and financial control too complex. For the time being, it would not be surprising if CSA or a similar approach was seen as a 'comfort blanket' to the directors in fulfilling their own responsibilities.

Auditors

As well as often being responsible for the internal audit function, the FD should be the first point of call for the external auditors. Chapter 15 talks of the importance of relationship management. I have found it highly valuable to establish and maintain an open and constructive dialogue with external auditors. The FD is not in a position to dictate anything to the auditors, but has a responsibility to ensure value for money from all the auditors, internal and external. One way is to secure a partnership whereby both groups sit down and agree a work programme which ensures the ability of the external auditors to meet their obligations and form an independent view, while optimising the joint resources available, avoiding duplication, and so on.

Auditors don't always get a good reception inside organisations. Again, the FD can smooth the way with management but also, auditors can do themselves favours. Of course sometimes it is necessary to pursue a particular course, but even external auditors, while they protect stakeholders' interests, can add real value to management with the work they do and the conclusions they reach. It is helpful for both audit and management to see auditors operating in the nature of internal consultants. They may have a routine programme, but this should be risk based and designed to afford management an understanding of where potential or actual weaknesses are present and where possible improvements may be made. The process can be greatly enhanced if auditors have a genuine understanding of the areas to be reviewed, give adequate notice of their proposed work and its purpose, enter a dialogue with managers before they commence and share their initial findings with managers informally first, thereby giving the opportunity for response and appropriate action before the report goes to a higher level.

The board does not expect to get a report on every detail of the audit and what was discovered. The FD and audit committee can help selectivity and prioritisation of issues while ensuring that all necessary action is already underway. Ideally the audit process should be non-confrontational at every stage. The FD has a key role to play in facilitating all of the above. In addition he or she can ensure that internal audit has a balanced, objective programme agreed in partnership with external audit, thereby minimising the external audit fee.

There are already a number of Standards in existence. All of these have some bearing on the auditors' and directors' responsibilities. While it is not the purpose of this report to go into technical detail, the FD has a responsibility to be aware of and understand the relevance of all these Standards, FRSs, etc. to ensure that the organisation complies. Again the importance of partnership is stressed. The auditors must know and understand all these and can advise the FD accordingly. In respect of the reporting requirements, the FD can ensure that the directors meet their responsibilities to show 'a true and fair view' and enable the external auditors to meet theirs, including reporting their findings and including responsibility statements in the accounts.

As with all other responsibilities related to the FD, the dictum of 'no surprises' applies to both sides. Last minute surprises can cost more than money. Fundamental to the efficiency of the process is regular, ongoing contact between the FD and the audit partner. Depending on the size of organisation, the FD may need to call on specialist support from time to time (e.g. tax, treasury or VAT advice). The auditors are invariably well placed to assist. In addition, if the FD fully understands the auditors' expectations of the detailed accounts, money can be saved by ensuring that all the work is done in-house, leaving only checking and confirmation to be completed. Contracting expert help may be cheaper than employing an underused internal resource.

Each looks to the other for assurance. The auditor, for the assurance of the directors that the accounts show a true and fair view, that effective accounting and control systems exist and that the stewardship of the assets, the viability and future of the organisation is intact. The FD, on behalf of the directors, can look for assurance of an efficient, cost-effective audit, risk-based and value-added, advising and guiding, rather than policing and directing. Where the dialogue between FD and auditor breaks down, everyone loses. As with the internal auditor, it need never be adversorial.

This book is neither about auditing nor the responsibilities of the auditor. Nevertheless, it is the responsibility of the FD and the audit committee to give the auditors the co-operation and assurance they need to perform their duties. Where directors or FDs are unhelpful or worse still evasive or deceitful, the matter becomes fraught.

> The audit function is sometimes seen to be an unnecessary drain on business finance but this is a very one-sided viewpoint. Audits are necessary to encourage and support vital investment which helps businesses to survive and expand. (Philip Shrives, May 1996, *Management Accounting*).

The greatest area of difficulty may be in SMEs, where the cost of audit may be proportionally larger, management expertise may be thinner on the ground and directors or owners may be more directive in their approach. If auditors are encouraged to perform their duties diligently and objectively, they should have little to fear. The FD is the prime agent in this process.

Compliance

Many organisations, such as financial services organisations, need to meet regulatory requirements. Depending on the scale, there would normally be an internal compliance function, which may often report through the internal auditor. Where the scale is small, the external auditor might be asked to perform the function. In general terms, there is a need to comply with many of the governance recommendations and standards etc., but there are many other areas, such as the Financial Services Act, the Yellow Book requirements (of the Stock Exchange), the Goode Committee, and so on, which have led to a growth in compliance as a separate function, again often reporting to or through the FD.

Assuming that for many organisations in both the private and public sector it will be business as usual, the partnership between the FD and the auditors is crucial. This does not mean that auditors need be complacent, however. Continuity of audit is desirable, but both from the point of view of costs and avoiding staleness and complacency, it may be valuable for the audit contract to be reviewed every three years, say or put out to contract if appropriate. The FD would lead this process and the audit committee would oversee it. It is increasingly the practice for organisations to outsource their internal audit as well.

Audit, internal efficiency, improvement and added value

It is many years since a judge pronounced that an auditor should be 'a watchdog, not a bloodhound'. Since then, forward thinking organisations have come to see the auditor more in the nature of a consultant. Although the fundamental routines of audit in checking and inspection of controls and verification of reports should never be dispensed with, these routines can uncover shortcomings which impede the organisation's efficiency. Even before embarking on re-engineering the corporation, a review of the existing processes and systems, to see if they are optimal and working in the way intended, could have dramatic effects on efficiency. Such an ongoing review could be an essential part of the work of the auditors, in a programme determined between the internal and external officers.

Audit should add value to management's understanding of the organisation and how it works. Often, only by reviewing how or why things have failed, can we discover ways to optimise or improve efficiency. It is no coincidence that auditors have increasingly used a risk based approach to audit. Apart from the improvement in the cost-effectiveness of the audit process, it is self-evident that the currency of auditors and managers is risk and that the consequences are always financial in some respect. Organisations make gains through actions which involve or acknowledge a degree of risk. Other things being equal, greater risk brings or demands greater returns and vice-versa. FDs should lead the process of weighing rewards against costs and risks. The auditor is a valuable partner in the process, before, during and after the event.

Risk management and corporate governance

Risk management and internal audit are converging. Both can be change agents. As it is not unusual for the FD to have responsibility for both these functions and treasury, there is real value in their partnership, complementarity or (in the case of audit and risk) combination. Both Hampel and Sir Sydney Lipworth, QC (in a recent address to the Association of Insurance and Risk Managers) would appear to agree.

> The UK's record on internal controls and prevention of risks over the past decade or so has not been exemplary...This is not to say that there has not been significant improvement in the governance environment since Cadbury. On the contrary, the whole area has improved dramatically. But they (Barings, Morgan Grenfell and others) highlight the ongoing need for vigilance and the necessity to avoid complacency.
>
> (*Source*: *Management Accounting*, January 1997).

Sir Sydney defined corporate governance as being for the purpose of ensuring that business is soundly and effectively managed, with risks being properly assessed and controlled.

Cadbury required the board to provide reasonable assurance of the reliability and integrity of the accounts and that the assets were safeguarded, that only authorised transactions were entered into, and that fraud and other irregularities were prevented and detected. 'But in practice, good corporate governance goes beyond that. Boards seek to satisfy themselves that all key risks faced by the company are identified, assessed, measured and controlled adequately – not concentrate solely on financial controls.' The FD, internal and external audit, compliance and the risk management function all combine in this responsibility. The FD may directly or indirectly manage them all.

One of the greatest areas of risk to an organisation's performance and viability is fraud. With the scale of growth and the advent of widespread use of the Internet, this ranks alongside derivatives, year 2000 and the Euro, as major areas of challenge right now and for the foreseeable future for the FD and the board, especially for SMEs.

Fraud

In 'The Picture in 2015' (*Accountancy* June 1995), Michael Hughes of BZW wrote:

> Financial fraud will continue to impose a burden on the reputation and balance sheets of companies and financial institutions around the world. Individuals and institutions will continue to be defrauded. Advances in telecommunications and automation, the globalisation of financial services and the wider use of electronic money will create additional challenges for regulatory and enforcement agencies.

There is no reason to modify this statement. Indeed, with the maturing of the Internet, the challenges have grown. Hacking has become more sophisticated and widespread and systems appear more open. Broadly, computer crime can be broken into three parts:

- fraud and theft;
- malicious acts (damage to systems and viruses);
- and misguided acts of moral rectitude (where hackers break into a system to prove how vulnerable it is).

In a 1996 Mori survey commissioned by *Security Gazette* and *Control Risks*, more than two-thirds of FDs from a random sample of the top 1000 companies in the UK said their companies had been the victims of serious fraud by employees. The survey also concluded that 'fraud is rife in business' and 'more often than not, corrupt practices are being perpetrated by those best able to prevent them: directors and managers....the threat of fraud is a key item on board-meeting agendas.'

Whatever the explanation for the apparent upsurge mentioned above (e.g. diminished job security), there has never been a more propitious time to commit fraud but there is also every possibility of preventing and detecting it. Of course if someone is determined to steal, they will find a way, but some of these frauds run into millions of pounds.

So in general, what are the circumstances that allow fraud to occur and what can the FD do to minimise the chances? In my view, there are two main reasons why fraud occurs: inadequate or non-existent controls, and the advent of sophisticated computer systems in an environment where insufficient managers have made the effort to understand them and how they work or to install controls in and around the systems at the time of design and implementation. Systems are always wanted in a hurry, especially financial systems. Time taken building in controls or asking the auditors to review the level of security before they are installed is too often seen as slowing down delivery or adding to cost. Once systems are in, insufficient attention is paid to protecting them. Even procedures such as the use of passwords, prevention of unauthorised access, virus and data integrity checks, prevention of introducing unauthorised software or hardware to the network are too often ignored.

The principle of separation of function can be applied wherever money is involved. Whether as manager, head of audit or director, the FD is best placed to ensure that procedures exist to minimise the possibility of fraud, check for evidence of fraud and corruption, report on the incidence of fraud to the audit committee and the board, and recommend appropriate steps to remedy the situation. Fraud and theft by employees are a major drain on corporate profits. In retailing, theft of stock can take a few percentage points out of net margins.

Conclusion

I have worked in the private and public sectors, for charities and non-profit organisations. There is inadequacy in all sectors if you look hard enough, but the best practice in any sector is transferable to others, irrespective of the stakeholders or the financial or regulatory regime. Governance should be a common language and practice and the consistent link from one to another is potentially the FD whose skills, experience and judgement in the field of governance should be common currency in all sectors.

The other link is the auditor. In partnership, the FD, the auditor and the non-executive directors hold the key to governance, especially through the audit committee.

10

The FD as planning manager

Following the lessons of over expansion in the late 1980s and the subsequent recession, investors and businesses have generally focused on the need for better financial management and control. However, businesses also need to achieve satisfactory returns and in today's circumstances can only thrive by reacting strategically to the rapid competitive change in a dynamic international environment with reduced regulatory barriers to entry. The challenge to Finance is to find ways to help their businesses to effectively balance and achieve the needs of these conflicting demands. (Keith Hamill, 1995, Finance Director, Forte plc).

As the table in Chapter 2 shows, FDs are expected to take increasing responsibility for strategic planning. This is a natural extension of the FD's traditional role, for as well as leading the corporate budgetary process, the FD should have responsibility for financial evaluation of the business plan, (although the planning manager may often manage the process whereby the figures are produced). It is not unusual therefore for the FD to be responsible for directing all the strategic planning processes of the organisation. Business plans often result in the need to obtain or rebalance the financing of the organisation, especially where major developments or acquisitions are involved.

The time frame for strategic planning was typically five years. Now it would often be three years. How can one define the strategic planning period? It could be said by some to be the period for which major capital or project investment could safely be planned. In the age of rapid technological obsolescence and global competition, however, it is not unusual for projects to be required to pay back over twelve or as little as six months. Some have also said that strategic planning is an irrelevance, because of the rapid pace of change.

Every organisation needs a focus, however. This would have two fundamental aspects: what is our mission? and what business are we in? (business focus). The 1980s made this unclear. Companies became so diversified that they lost their focus. Now a growing number are disaggregating (BTR, Thorn-EMI, Hanson, ICI/Zeneca, etc.). Meanwhile, others are trying to grow even bigger on the grounds that they are global players. In every market, this is leaving opportunities for smaller companies to create a niche for themselves.

I have described the outline of management processes elsewhere. It starts with direction. In strategic planning, this includes:

- mission;
- vision;
- values;

- goals;

- review of the market(s) and the environment in which the organisation operates;

- SWOT analysis;

- determining critical success factors;

- setting key performance indicators.

Ideally, the FD who is responsible for strategic planning will design the process, collect together all the relevant data and information and then either facilitate the strategic planning process him or herself, or contract an impartial outsider to do so. Throughout the process, it is useful to be able to quantify or predict the possible consequences of proposed decisions, or the responses of competitors. The FD is well-equipped to handle this. Where the organisation is large enough, a dedicated planning manager is ideal, having a constant focus on strategy and implementation of the plan, including monitoring change and external challenges. The ideal strategic plan may be cast once a year, but will be capable of constantly evolving as the organisation manages for change.

There are two key messages for business and economics: attempts to predict and control the long term future are doomed to failure; the organisations most likely to survive in the long run are the ones that are most flexible and so best adapted to cope with unpredictable change. (Brian Singleton-Greene reviewing *Chaos, Management and Economics: the Implications of Non-Linear Thinking*, 1994, Parker & Stacey).

This does not necessarily invalidate business planning over the short term. The key is flexibility and adaptability, two characteristics which the modern FD needs, especially when leading the planning process. Where the function is not directed by the FD, there will often be a general manager reporting direct to the board for the planning function. In either case, there needs to be a close working relationship between the two. Each will involve every other department of the organisation in their work: the planning manager to plan or predict the future actions of the organisation, the FD, with the planning manager, to quantify the consequences of various courses of action and also to record and facilitate the comparison of actual with plan, to help determine possible remedial action.

Performance review

Planning is a continual process. It needs to be a participative team process. Reference has been made earlier to the continuous cycle of improvement. Normally this would be focused around a monthly review, but in the environment of constant change and challenge which faces every organisation, the process is ongoing. Response or remedial action cannot afford to wait for a month, because by then, it may be seven or eight weeks after the event which precipitated the need for change.

An integral part of the planning process is performance review. Without it, the plan is meaningless. There is a useful model which can be adopted by any organisation at any level, to afford the maximum benefit from this regular review. It is captured in the following questions (which can be applied to any similar situation in business or personal life):

- What was the plan?
- What was the actual outcome?
- What is the gap between plan and outcome?
- What are the reasons for the gap?
- What action is already underway to resolve the situation?

All too often it has been my experience that managers wait for the finance function to produce the monthly report and then set about finding out the reasons for what went wrong. The enterprising manager makes it his or her business to know what is going on all the time. Divergence from plan is picked up as soon as it happens. The manager will then ask the financial support for a quantification of the possible effects and courses of action and that action will already be under way by the time the report for that period is presented to top management.

Financial strategy, planning and reporting

> The finest plans are often spoilt through the pettiness of those who are supposed to carry them out, since even emperors can do nothing without the support of soldiers and hangers-on. (Berthold Brecht).

The FD has an inherent responsibility for financial strategy. As planner, the FD would be responsible for leading the development of overall business strategy also, which helps to optimise the financial direction and management. The ordered makeup of most FDs helps them to ensure that all the necessary components of the plan come together in a cohesive whole and that they are managed and reviewed as efficiently as possibly through the periodic review process. The periodic output of financial information to support that process should ideally be automated, so that the manager receives it either on an ongoing basis, or in real time.

This does not negate the need for the finance department to be available to help interpret the financial information as required. When problems arise in automated reporting procedures, if there is no process for interpretation or understanding and the information starts to diverge from the outcome expected by the manager, suspicions can begin to arise and eventually the manager may either repudiate or disown the outcomes, or, worse still, start to create his or her own reporting process.

The ideal is for the finance department to facilitate the development of reporting processes and systems under the control of the manager (as opposed to the traditional 'tablets of stone' approach). If those systems and processes are developed with the partnership and understanding of the manager, the whole organisation benefits in terms of teamwork and efficiency. The role of the finance function then becomes one of consultancy and support to the rest of the organisation, to facilitate understanding and the development of information systems. This ensures the organisation always has the ability to understand contemplated or historical actions, ensuring accountability and efficiency. While inevitably this leads to a reduction in the number of bean counters, it should also lead to an improvement in the quality of support at the centre and the decentralisation of accounting routines to the line. Response to change in a dynamic environment requires that managers are always up to date without having to wait weeks for the results.

Forecasting and modelling

Managers need fast, meaningful, ongoing information in order to manage proactively in an environment of perpetual change. The FD needs to conspire in change management rather than perfect microscopic analysis. If financial reporting can produce spurious accuracy, so can forecasting. As planning manager, the FD will be responsible for the provision of forecasts and models to inform the decision making process. It is not unusual to find models which exactly replicate the processes to produce the historical information. If this can be achieved economically, all well and good, but any model is only as reliable as its structure and the assumptions fed into it. These become less reliable the longer the period of the projections.

Forecasting is not budgeting:

> the primary difference between budgeting for financial management and
> forecasting for financial planning lies in the degree of detail – budgets for financial
> control will usually be much more detailed than forecasts; the purpose – budgeting
> is generally for control whereas forecasting is primarily for information; the
> interested parties who, in the case of forecasts, are as likely to be outside the
> company as inside. (Michael Lawson in *The New Manager's Handbook*, 1990).

'What If?'

> A theory has only the alternative of being right or wrong. A model has a third
> possibility – it may be right but irrelevant. (Manfred Eigen).

More useful than a spurious prediction is a scenario planning approach – 'what if'
analysis. Modelling the past allows the FD to quantify the possible effects of different
courses of action. Forecasts derived from the organisation's environment, together with a
realistic SWOT analysis, can be combined with the possible outcomes to determine the
optimal course of action.

Scenario planning is not new and not always used by companies. It can be
time-consuming and expensive if the whole of the top team is involved, and it does not
appeal to the more scientific or practical members of the team. However, some major
organisations like Shell have put it to good effect. FDs tend by nature to be practical and
in an environment of constant change and chaos, may conclude that long term strategic
planning or scenario analysis are not appropriate. Nevertheless, the ability to evaluate
various possibilities helps to formulate strategy, and also to cope with the unexpected.
The FD as planning manager has to find a way of balancing the short with the longer
term, the possible and the fanciful with the present and the practicable.

As well as scenario planning and the review of various possible options for the core plan
of the organisations, many of those options will involve major developments or capital
expenditure. The FD will be responsible not only for helping evaluate the options, but also
often for the financing and acquisition of those developments. The use of business cases
is now mandatory in most parts of the public sector because of growing, competing
demands for capital. Here, not only the organisation but also the entire industry needs a
common set of measures to evaluate competing projects.

Benchmarking

Before leaving the subject of planning, it is relevant to discuss benchmarking. Benchmarking is undoubtedly a macro factor. It is based on comparing your organisation with class-leading, or ideally world class, comparable organisations. Benchmarking means learning about your own processes and practices, learning about the comparable processes and practices in other organisations and making the necessary holistic improvements to enable you to match or beat the best in the world. It works best as part of a TQM programme and a process of continuous improvement, because if you pick the very best, by the time you have reached their standard, they will already have moved on. This does not necessarily mean that you benchmark your entire organisation against others. Xerox is credited with pioneering benchmarking, to try and counter the Japanese threat. What Xerox did was to benchmark each integral part of the business against the best in class for that aspect.

Other organisations, such as ICL, which have introduced benchmarking as part of a holistic quality programme, have set their standard against, say, the upper quartile of a particular group. The strategic importance of benchmarking is such that the relevant analysis is likely to be incorporated into the SWOT and goal-setting processes. The particular relevance to FDs is not just where they are leading the strategic planning process. Also, benchmarking will affect the chosen performance indicators at an organisational, divisional or process level. It goes without saying that apart from benchmarking financial performance, the finance function itself could do worse than to benchmark its financial planning, management, reporting and accounting processes against the best in class. This could be done with the help of one's auditors for example. It is not unusual for industry specific accounting firms to conduct confidential benchmarking exercises which the participants can share.

The KPIs for an organisation may very well be influenced by benchmarking, for if the comparable measures have been carefully chosen, they can be equally appropriate for the absolute or year to year assessment of performance. They need not be immediately obvious. For example, a building society might use customer retention as a KPI. It may be possible for you to find an equally relevant key measure in your own organisation, which goes beyond the traditional financial ratios, but because of the factors it captures and the consequences it connotes, is an excellent all-round measure of performance. If you accept the proposal that a quality organisation will get and keep quality customers, then it must be appropriate to find at least one key measure which not only captures the quality of process or customer relationship, but can be used as a genuine industrial or inter-industrial sector benchmark. The very best organisations use trans-sector measures, such as quality of product, customer complaints and retention.

11

The FD as corporate finance manager

In looking forward to future years, organisations have to budget within their expected means. Once they establish that they wish to continue with the core business and when they have forecast the achievable volumes, the consequent costs can be determined. Over and above that, it may be possible or desirable to invest in the future. Broadly these investments could fall into two general categories: business improvements and business developments. Part of the FD's role is to guide the organisation on the consequences of each, in terms of outcome and financing required. As mentioned earlier, the FD may also be involved in preparing or leading business plans or business cases as appropriate.

The next priority after the core business should be business improvements. These would be investments to improve the efficiency of the things the organisation already does. Such investments should produce a very rapid payback. Beyond this, and in keeping with the longer term strategy, there may be a long list of potential developments, i.e. things which are new to the organisation. These may involve acquisitions, startups, development of new product lines, and so on. The FD would be closely involved in guiding the management team on the choices available, those that merit consideration and those which should be discarded. Wearing the planner's hat also, the FD will ensure that the organisation does not contemplate anything which does not fit with the agreed strategic direction, or does not provide a payback within a reasonable period. These payback periods are shrinking as a result of rapid change and lowering barriers to entry, largely as technology progresses.

Investment appraisal

In many textbooks this topic would be called capital project evaluation, or similar. All investments involve capital, whether derived from internal cash flow or external funding. Investment implies an action to deliver benefits for the future. The word investment has a positive connotation. Yet many investments are not tested against the corporate strategy for fit, are not subject to rigorous or meaningful cost-benefit analysis and, most important, are not subject to post-implementation review. For the present purposes, I am going beyond the usual capital project to cover all investments, because they should be subject to the same consistent disciplines of analysis and review. The FD may not lead or carry out all the appraisals, but has a responsibility for consistency of method across the organisation. The FD could be deemed responsible for ensuring that the organisation's overall return on capital can be achieved. The FD may give guidance on hurdle rates, for example, but even these may need to differ in different parts of the organisation. For example, very few IT investments would clear the corporate hurdle rate.

I do not propose to discuss capital appraisal methods in detail. It is for the organisation to decide, on the advice of the FD, how to proceed. However, some observations will be made in passing. The FD may be involved in both the main aspects of investment: determining and evaluating possible investments and determining how best to finance them. In the former case the FD would be acting as planner/financial manager, in the latter as treasurer. Financing involves intermediating between sources and uses of finance. Usually the sources are outside the organisation, but in the case of internally generated funds or complex organisations, the sources may be within the company.

> The prosperity of a business depends more on its ability to create profitable investment opportunities than on its ability to appraise them. (Pike & Dobbins, 1986).

Why is investment important? It renews or enriches existing revenue streams, delivers new revenue streams or improves the cost or operating efficiency of the organisation. It should be seen to improve long term stakeholder value: increased shareholder value, better, cheaper products for customers, better rewards and security for employees, a stronger brand or reputation in the public eye.

The rate of return on a project can be measured against the weighted cost of capital, to determine whether there is a payback (i.e. increase in shareholder value). Hurdle rates will vary according to the level of risk involved. It should never be forgotten that money has a time value and therefore, common practice is to use net present value (NPV) to measure the incremental real value, or internal rate of return (IRR) to determine the breakeven financing rate which needs to be exceeded to make a contribution. Some people will go further and conduct a sensitivity analysis for various levels of sales etc. and this may even be taken to the sophisticated heights of probability analysis. Spurious accuracy can be achieved, however and it is not recommended that management casts around until a method is found that gives the right answer. Good projects pass all the tests.

The FD is often the best judge of whether a project meets and is likely to deliver against the required targets. The test for the FD in future, however, will come from change and volatility in the competitive environment and the need for flexibility. Traditional hurdle rates of return need to fall in a low inflation environment. At any one time, there will be a number of competing projects. The skill is to balance:

- the short with the long term;
- the customer project with the support project;
- core business improvements with new developments;

- business as usual with innovation;

- hard facts with blind faith, etc.

FDs as members of the wider team will need to see the broader values, rather than just stop projects in their tracks with black and white analysis. After all this, prioritisation and balance will still leave the FD having to ensure the protection or development of long term value.

Pike and Dobbins identify four main groups of investment:

- capital projects (which might be scale or quality improvements);

- replacement projects;

- working capital investment (if it is an investment rather than tying up funds);

- mergers and acquisitions (and, increasingly, strategic alliances).

Different projects will require different volumes and types of financing (e.g. equity, borrowing, leasing, etc.). The FD will often intermediate the finance and should certainly advise on the mix, the gearing and the dividend policy of the organisation. One area of investment which is often overlooked but should be part of the fundamental strategic planning processes of the organisation, is stopping doing things. This can produce better returns than doing new things and releases capital to finance other things. How many organisations ask themselves the questions:

- If we were building this organisation from scratch, what would we do differently?

- What are we doing that we do not need to do?

- What would be the consequences if we stopped doing this?

Questions like these can lead to disinvestment by sale or closure, demerger, etc. The FD can ask these questions. The FD can also ask whether previous projects are delivering their forecast benefits at the expected level of costs.

Investment appraisal and planning for growth also seem to me to have changed largely as a result of the movement towards managing for shareholder value. The capital asset pricing model and the weighted average cost of capital are concepts which no longer seem to reside only in text books. The heady 80s have given way to the cautious 90s but shareholder value still drives companies towards making investments and financing themselves aggressively if still prudently. The FD is the long stop in ensuring that the appropriate balance is struck and that major mistakes are not made. (R N Chisman, 1995, Financial Director, Stakis plc).

Projects and finance

The FD may sometimes be responsible for leading or directing major projects. Even where this is not the case, there will be a key support role to be played in providing or supporting the financial evaluation and ongoing review and often in arranging the project or corporate finance to afford the development. Information systems, major capital projects and mergers, acquisitions and disposals could all require substantial finance. Wearing the treasurer's hat, the FD might well be involved in raising this finance. Often the FD may have responsibility for the information systems function. In this case, the FD would be responsible for sponsoring the investment as well. Where the organisation adopts the approach of having board members lead the steering group for a departmental information systems proposal, it would not be unusual for the FD to take the role of chair, because of the essential impartiality of the role.

Asset finance can be a very complex subject. Within the FD's core role should be the management of the financing of the organisation, whether or not it has a separate treasury function. The latter may effect the financing or funding transactions, but the FD should take the strategic lead on the optimum financing structure, its timing and composition. Very often with the acquisition of capital assets or new businesses, the financing will be influenced or dictated by the nature or duration of the purchase. For example, if an asset/liability management approach is adopted, the duration of the finance would be matched to the expected duration of the asset.

Mergers and acquisitions

The mergers and acquisitions (M&A) process might include the following steps:

- identifying possibilities;
- evaluating possible targets;
- selecting targets;
- acquiring a target;
- rationalising the acquisition or merger;
- accounting for the acquisition or merger.

This is a simplified process. While it is ideal to initiate and carry through a dialogue with a possible target, sometimes the bid is treated as hostile. This substantially increases the work involved, the costs and the risk of failure. Although this passage on M&A is largely directed to quoted companies, many of the points will be of relevance to all mergers. In all cases, the FD would be expected to play a key role, if not to lead many of the processes.

Strategic planning may lead to an acquisitions strategy as part of business development. Identifying possible targets should be conditioned by a clear view of what business you are in and how possible acquisitions fit. Normally a set of criteria would be drawn up and a long list of targets prepared against these. In evaluating possible targets for selection, the FD would look at the track record after having reviewed the accounting and reporting practices to determine whether performance needs restating in the same terms as the acquiring company. A review of markets, customers, distribution, suppliers, products, strengths and weaknesses, financial structure and strength, accounting practices, opportunities to reduce, resource or sell off unwanted assets, etc., may all be part of the process. It would make sense to use researchers to have conversations with some of the key partners mentioned above.

These are only a fraction of the considerations in what is a massive exercise. When a particular target has been selected, eventually a due diligence exercise will need to be carried out. The FD would direct this. Year 2000 will become a major factor, as a growing number of prospective bids fail, due to non-compliance by the target company.

Fair value in acquisitions

The main reason for making an acquisition should be to enhance long term value without damage to the core, the brand, etc. If all the detailed analysis produces no reasons against proceeding, the price must be decided. This is difficult. Especially if there is a possibility of resistance or competition from another bidder, there may be two prices in mind – an opening bid and the maximum price you are prepared to pay. It is important to see and justify the value in a bid but it is even more important to deliver or derive that value after merger.

The first consideration is whether the price/earnings ratio of the target is higher than the predator. If so, then unless other value can be derived post-merger, it will dilute the earnings of the predator and therefore reduce long term value. It is too easy to end up overpaying where there is a contested bid, or in a merger where the other party extracts expensive promises, such as a no redundancy agreement, golden handshakes, etc. On the other hand, it is sometimes possible to find and release additional values after acquisition which were not expected in the pre-acquisition review.

Especially for quoted companies, the costs of acquisition can be very high. The FD plays a key role throughout the acquisition process and therefore a large amount of financial management resource will be used before, during and afterwards. This is true to varying degrees of other parts of the organisation. Outside advisers will invariably be needed and, especially if the bid is contested or fails, the costs can threaten the original rationale for proceeding. VSEL was subject to contested bids from GEC and British Aerospace. GEC topped BAe's all share bid with a 'knockout' cash bid and for a while, shareholders were concerned that BAe might be tempted higher to a level where value would be diluted. BAe's share price rose ten per cent when the board decided not to proceed.

Here as in most aspects of M&A, the FD should play an important role, not a negative check on the process but a review and reference point, constructively challenging whether the originally agreed parameters are still in place. If not, then a review may lead to the acquisition being abandoned. Far more acquisitions do not proceed, especially before the bid, than proceed to fruition. A cool head is needed. A final concern is that the huge and growing amount of resource involved as the bid proceeds can lead to 'the eye off the ball' and potential short term damage to the core business. Sometimes it can take some time to recover from the anticlimax after a failed bid.

After the merger or acquisition there is the need or opportunity to rationalise the two businesses. This is an exercise which should proceed as quickly as possible. Loss of momentum can lead to underachievement of economies or values. Some mergers had not been completed five years after the original date (especially merging the cultures). This would be a source of great concern to the FD because all these factors cost money. It is advisable to write off as much of the extraordinary costs as possible and allowable, as quickly as possible. This clears the decks so that the future values can be clearly seen as they are delivered.

This brings me to the matter of accounting for M&A. For a long time the position has been unclear and unsatisfactory. Although there was an accounting standard in place (SSAP 23), different practices had led to difficulty in seeing the true values or otherwise after merger. This made matters particularly difficult for intercompany comparison. It has also been difficult to rely on earnings figures, which are already confused by different practices on goodwill and depreciation. Differential accounting for acquisitions is a very good reason for moving to cashflow as a means of valuing companies rather than earnings (see Chapter 6). Now we have FRS 6 (*Acquisitions and Mergers*) and FRS 7 (*Fair Values in Acquisition Accounting*) which it is hoped will clear the picture somewhat. All this adds to the technical burden for the FD and increasing reliance on external auditors for advice.

Bid defence

Matters become even more complicated for M&A if the target company decides to defend against the bid. Many FDs would do well to prepare a set of processes and line up a defence adviser against the possibility of a bid. If you go through the exercise once, maintain a brief and review the procedures from time to time, you are more likely to succeed in your defence. This can also be very expensive. This hardly seems fair if you did not welcome the bid in the first place, but in the US there was a period when 'spoiling' bids were a common occurrence, with companies deliberately 'softened up' by having to go through a defence process and be diverted from their core business.

There are some tactics the company can adopt to try and ward off a predator, e.g.:

- seeking a reference to the Monopolies and Mergers Commission;
- demerging (breaking up) the company;
- MBO (management buyout) of all or part of the business;
- seeking a 'white knight'.

If a bid fails, first time round, the predator may not make another approach for at least twelve months. This was the case in Enterprise/Lasmo and Trafalgar House/Northern Electric. The circumstances were unusual in the latter case because of the intervention of the regulator to review prices during the bid process. The target company can invite the predator to submit a new bid within twelve months. This did not happen with Northern Electric, although it was later taken over by another party.

> Accounting for acquisition has long been seen as fertile ground for manipulating figures. (David Tweedie, 1994, Chairman, Accounting Standards Board).

Corporate finance and funding sources

The corporate finance markets have exploded in growth in the last twenty years. Many of the aspects have almost become industries in themselves. The ways in which a company can access finance for development or expansion are increasing steadily, as is the availability of funds. Nowhere is this more true than with venture capital.

Among the FD's choices available for finance are:

- self-generated cash;

- grants;

- bank facilities and loans of various kinds;

- corporate bonds;

- venture capital;

- business 'angels';

- AIM or a full Stock Market listing;

- being acquired.

The amount of venture capital available has grown enormously in recent years, to the extent that some of it is chasing deals. A venture capitalist will typically take an equity stake in the business, but may build in the ability for management to buy back or earn back that stake. The best known source of such funds is 3i, which became so successful that it floated on the Stock Exchange itself, after its founding owners (some of the clearing banks) wanted to demerge their investment.

'Business angels' are often high net worth individuals prepared to speculate with cash. What these, venture capitalists, AIM and the stock market have in common is the dependence they place on the quality of management (especially the chairman, CEO and FD) and the NEDs, and the clarity of focus, especially on what management needs the capital for. Anyone coming to the market just to sell their stake will get short shrift. Increasingly, with all forms of investment which involve outsiders taking a stake in the equity or even buying the whole company, they will insist on key managers remaining to manage the business. Goodwill is not enough on its own to make the deal work.

The 1980s and 1990s saw the growth of MBOs, leveraged buyouts (LBOs) and, latterly, MBIs and investor buyouts (IBOs). The latter is sometimes known as a bought deal. MBOs, very popular in the early 1990s, slumbered in the mid-1990s as some did not work out and greater risks were perceived than had been first assumed. With so many funds chasing a good home and the corporate governance strictures placed on the directors of the selling company, it is no surprise that more 'auctions' have been conducted, leading to higher prices and greater risks. This seems to have escaped HMG's processes, the most alarming example being Porterbrook (the privatised rolling stock leasing company), sold off by the government in January 1996 for £525m, only to be bought by Stagecoach six months later for £827m. One manager made a profit of almost £37m!

Self-generation may be the cheapest form of capital, but if you follow the Stern Stuart EVA school of thinking, you should fund from debt, especially corporate bonds. Indeed, some see the potential growth of a huge UK 'junk bond' market, when the interest cost is set against the availability of funds at quite a low credit rating. Failing this, conventional loans or bank facilities would be appropriate.

The company bankers will be a critical factor in any form of funding. It will be necessary to have a clear plan and the support of one's bankers to succeed. Nowhere is this more true than in the case of flotation. The purpose of flotation should be primarily to raise capital for development or investment purposes. Indeed the investors will want to be clear what the funds will be used for, otherwise they could cause deterioration of net returns and dilution of earnings if they simply sit in the bank. Investors will not be impressed if the owners simply want to raise money to get out of the business at the top of its business cycle. This is where due diligence comes in.

The whole process of flotation is complex, time consuming and relatively expensive. AIM may cost a fraction of a full listing and can be achieved in as little as six weeks (although four or five months is more the norm). The planning process would need to start at least a year before that, however, and the preparations will be onerous to some companies.

There is so much to do that it can stop the management processes in their tracks with quite a small enterprise, especially if it takes its eye off the ball. The due diligence process is designed to ensure that all is as it seems and the group of lawyers and advisors have the duty to protect the interests of incoming investors – a process which is replicated for mergers and acquisitions, IBOs, MBOs, MBIs, venture capital, etc.

There will always be a huge amount of tidying up to do in preparation for flotation: contracts, IPR, systems, etc. Then the round of PR and presentations will consume huge amounts of especially the FD's time (who would be expected to lead the capital process, alongside the chairman and chief executive). Prospective investors, analysts, journalists and fund managers could be included in the round, especially for a highly visible transaction.

Obviously, borrowing or venture capital will be the only routes open to many SMEs, but whatever route is used, the FD will need to assure investors that the company has a clear strategy, a carefully prepared case, especially as to the needs and prospective use of the capital. Even more so, the judgement will be made on the management, rather than the company or its products. The former may need to be augmented or even replaced, including new, credible NEDs.

Valuation

The methods of valuation for companies, whether being acquired or seeking capital, are still open to debate. They are usually either asset or income based. In the former case, net realisable value (NRV) is most common, but income bases produce more generous values, especially where the asset base is poor. Here, the present value of future revenues streams, a dividend valuation, or, more usually, P/E ratio will be more common. In reality, however, many bids fail because the management or owners value the company higher than anyone is prepared to pay.

12

The FD as change manager

> Corporate change – rebuilding, if you will – has parallels to the most ambitious and perhaps most noble of the plastic arts, architecture. The skill of corporate leaders, the ultimate change masters, lies in their ability to envision a new reality and aid in its translation into concrete terms.....Change involves the crystallisation of new action possibilities (new policies, new behaviours, new patterns, new methodologies, new products, or new market ideas) based on reconceptualised patterns in the organisation. (Kanter, 1985).

> The future holds many uncertainties, but looking ahead there is one thing of which I am sure. Change...is here to stay. I will go further than that. Change is going to come about ever faster and more frequently....What it means to business is quite clear to me. Those who are best able to manage change have the best prospects for success. Those who are unable to manage change are unlikely to survive. (Sir Colin Marshall, in the foreword to *Ignition*, 1992, Chaudry-Lawton & Lawton).

Ms Kanter is still professor at Harvard. Sir Colin Marshall needs no introduction. What is significant is that both these comments will remain indefinitely relevant. Change is not just a passing fad as some would have it. It is unfortunate that TQM and process re-engineering have been perceived as such, as part of the guru culture which pervades modern management thinking.

Change is the only constant. Corporations will have to re-engineer themselves ceaselessly in order to remain competitive (not merely in order to cut costs). A total quality approach is the only way for corporations to survive well into the 21st century (except in an imperfect market). Downsizing to cut costs has been shown to be a 'black hole' strategy. As the corporation continues to shrink in order to sustain profitability and shareholder returns, it must eventually reach the point where it might as well shut down and pay back the capital. The dramatic growth of cash distributions by quoted companies will escalate. Starting with disaggregation by MBOs and separate floats, the pattern of organisation is moving steadily to the federalist view revived by Charles Handy.

> We have to find another way, by changing the structure of our institutions to give more power to the small and the local. We have to do that, with all the untidiness which it entails, while still looking for efficiency, and the benefits of co-ordination and control. More is needed, therefore, than good intentions, to 'empower' the individual to do what we want him or her to do. The structures and the systems have to change, to reflect a new balance of power. That means federalism. (Handy, 1994).

Wherever you look, in public or private sector, inside or outside organisations, you see a pattern emerging, of empowering and associating smaller, more flexible, autonomous business units. All these units need information, fast and reliable, to determine the current position and make the decisions continually demanded to facilitate the ongoing change necessary to keep up with competition and evolving customers' needs. Whether these autonomous units are in, or associated with, a larger entity, the FD faces two immediate challenges: the need to be adaptable, flexible and responsive to the information needs of the parts and the whole; and the need to be able to consolidate the whole for external or public reporting purposes.

People, processes and systems

The evolving, adapting strategic plan and change are delivered through three mediums; people, processes and systems – in that order:

- people make and share decisions;

- processes are designed and redesigned in order to implement them efficiently and effectively, in keeping with the customers' changing needs;

- systems should be designed and exist only for the purpose of supporting the processes through which people implement the decisions.

> To achieve their objectives, cope with change...managers need to learn how to manage themselves, which involves: understanding the nature of management work...understanding the management processes...practising and developing the skills of management required to ensure that these processes operate effectively...Managers must also understand how to work with other people, which involves working in groups, managing change, and the use of communicating and interpersonal skills...Additionally, they must learn how to work in the organisation, which means understanding about organisation structure and development, organisation culture, the different functions within businesses, and the strategic planning process...Finally, managers have to learn how to work with the various stakeholders of the organisation. (Armstrong, 1997).

All these themes are relevant to the FD, almost above all. The FD is not only one of the most senior and highly visible general managers in the organisation, but is also responsible for leading the financial (and often management) information processes, which capture and convey to business managers the ongoing consequences of their business decisions.

It was easier in the good old days of course. Organisations were structured, bureaucratic and rigid, managed through functional 'chimneys' up which information had to flow in order to pass to its neighbours. Information could be collected centrally, organised, analysed and ordered, before being distributed on a 'need to know' basis, sometimes weeks after it was useful. This will no longer do, without running the risk of strangling the organisation. Structures need to be flexible and adaptable to respond to change. Management processes need to be fluid, formal and informal information is needed immediately, to inform decisions and reflect consequences, in order continually to adapt.

We shall return to the subject of processes in the next chapter. The most obvious impact of change is on the people in an organisation. So how do we manage people? How do we create an environment where people's natural talent can flourish? This is a question for the FD to ask, no less than any other manager, for themselves, for their colleagues and team members, for the people with whom they interact and especially in the many situations where the FD is also managing the HR or personnel function (e.g. in many SMEs).

Organisation

If we were rebuilding the organisation from scratch, to deliver the current strategic plan, let alone to allow its shape to evolve to take account of constant change, would we build it the way it is? Probably not. Business process re-engineering has come in for a bad press. Why – because, starting in the US, it was used as a device, or an excuse, to cut costs, through downsizing. The result has been that hardly any corporations have delivered lasting, positive change. Many had to return to the exercise more than once. Certainly, costs came down and for a time the shareholders were happy, but in the process, somewhere along the line, other key stakeholders were forgotten – customers and employees. Even though BPR followed much later in the UK and was less widely practised than across the Atlantic, we now have a business environment where, despite the recovery in the economy, employees and managers are frightened, mistrustful, demotivated, overworked and stressed out.

> Re-engineering, properly, is the fundamental rethinking and radical redesign of business processes to achieve dramatic improvements in critical, contemporary measures of performance, such as cost, quality, service, and speed....re-engineering is not restructuring or downsizing. These are just fancy terms for reducing capacity to meet current, lower demand....downsizing and restructuring only mean doing less with less. Re-engineering, by contrast, means

> doing *more* with less....Re-engineering also is not the same as reorganizing, delayering, or flattening the organisation, although re-engineering may, in fact, produce a flatter organisation. (Hammer & Champy, 1994).

So what has been happening? In possibly the deepest recession this century, corporations found it easier to cut back production to meet lower demand, than to seek to create new demand. Middle management was deemed to be unproductive and cut away like so much dead wood. Communication may have become easier, costs may have fallen, but far from achieving empowerment, demotivation and disillusionment abounded in a workforce that felt either threatened, guilty (for their departed colleagues), or both. There was no long term contract any more. Meanwhile, a huge amount of intellectual capital went with the departing middle managers, grey hairs became redundant, in favour of a new, brasher, more energetic workforce. Now the grey hairs are being sought again, to add wisdom and experience to youth and innovation.

The FD as change manager

Much of the foregoing not only indicates a whole new set of challenges for the FD of tomorrow, but also a completely new way of working. In all walks of management, progressive organisations have for some time been dispensing with the services of managers and staff of all ages who cannot adapt to the new ways of managing. This change will accelerate, not only as individuals fall by the wayside, lacking the appropriate skills or will to change, but also as organisations join the quality revolution and take on a completely new way of working and adapting. Technology will not be the only engine of change, although of course as organisations look for efficiencies to remain competitive, it will be easy to replace humans with machines to perform routine tasks. In due course the main engine of change will be the processes of managing and delivering themselves. New skills will be sought and developed. All organisations will need to be quality organisations, the leaders will be visionaries.

Vision and leadership

Vision and leadership skills will increasingly be demanded of all managers. As the finance department becomes less of a number crunching machine and more of a high quality team of specialists and advisers to the organisation, broader management capability will become at least as important as numeracy. Most of the department will be working most of the time with outsiders or multidisciplinary teams across the organisation, rather than up and down the organisation. The FD will not be able to operate as an autocratic line manager but will need to work as a team leader and facilitator in a number of processes which involve cross sections of different disciplines: projects, planning, communication, etc.

> Leadership, like everything in life that is vital, finds its source in understanding. To be worthy of management responsibility today, a man must have insight into the human heart, for unless he has an awareness of human problems, a sensitivity towards the hopes and aspirations of those whom he supervises, and a capacity for analysis of the emotional forces that motivate their conduct, the projects entrusted to him will not get ahead no matter how often wages are raised. (Clarence B Randall).

The FD as leader

Nothing in this book is meant to imply that there are not FDs with outstanding people and process management skills, including leadership qualities. Certainly the business environment is changing and evolving and a new breed is emerging. Many always had the capability in a time when it might have seemed 'soft' to display creativity and caring, as opposed to driving and diligence. Some people have believed the convention that leaders are born, not made. Personally, I believe that most people have leadership potential and every team needs this.

Every good FD should be able to demonstrate excellence in personal and interpersonal skills. Such a requirement is no less true of all general managers. If they cannot lead people, skilfully, in teams and by example, for what potential damage and demotivation might they be responsible? Management today is more about enabling and empowering than leading in the traditional assumed sense. As teams come together for specific purposes, listening is as important as directing and every team member needs the potential to lead the team process in their own area of responsibility or expertise.

The FD of today, let alone tomorrow, needs:

- organisational skills as well as technical ability;
- strategic, thinking, analysis, problem-solving and decision making skills;
- people skills and relationship management skills to work skilfully and responsively with all the organisation's stakeholders;
- self-management and personal effectiveness.

No organisation can optimise its success without realising that it exists primarily to understand and meet customers' needs. The organisation and its strategy should be designed solely for the customer purpose. The job of the FD is to inform of the consequences of various alternative ways of achieving this and delivering long term value to shareholders. There are two sides to the profit equation – sales and costs. By all means improve cost efficiency, but not at the expense of sales. Keep cutting away the cost base and the organisation will shrink. For a while it may be more profitable, but unless it is capable of fundamentally re-inventing itself, eventually the overhead will swamp the profit.

Flatter organisations may be less costly, but they are self-defeating if they result in permanently demotivated employees and have critical gaps in the management and business processes. Flat may be a convenient way to think of the efficient organisation, in cost and communication terms, but flexible, adaptable, designed for purpose and capable of constantly re-inventing itself for that evolving purpose is more important. Finally, in order to understand the value of all these approaches, where better to start than in the finance department, which is all overhead.

New skills – flexibility and adaptability

> Never discourage anyone who continually makes progress, no matter how slow. (Plato).

Management in general will increasingly have to reflect adaptability and flexibility to manage different teams in the new environment. The FD will find this change as difficult as anyone. Anyone aspiring to high office will need to undergo a wide variety of management skills training but also demonstrate the ability to apply the skills acquired. Because of the traditionally narrow characteristics possessed by many accountants, they have often been left to operate in a narrow specialist way. Not all accountants make good managers (or vice-versa) but every good accountant can acquire an understanding of what good management is about. In situations where they cannot apply those skills themselves, they will understand enough to know they should seek support elsewhere.

In order to add optimum value to the organisation, modern FDs should understand all modern theory and practice, for their new role is to advise, guide and support – facilitate the delivery of the strategic plan, not hold it back. They must be team players and part of that team role is to lead the way in constructive, value generating activities and to facilitate the optimum financial information processes to meet the strategic need.

Based on my experience, when the FD leads in this way, change happens faster, because we have been expected too often in the past to bring up the rear and hold innovation back with conservative, anachronistic practices and systems. Finally, many FDs, especially in SMEs or even larger organisations now carry the personnel function in their portfolio. My own view is that there should ideally be a HR director. If not, it is the duty of the FD, working with appropriate support from peers and the support team, to seek to achieve the same ideal strategic, empowering people processes.

The FD as people manager

Everything in this chapter can help the organisation to achieve sharper focus, better corporate success and a more empowered culture. It also gives the FD insights into the optimum processes of people management, in order to understand, support and facilitate these where appropriate (especially where the people role is combined with that of FD). Much of this understanding can be put to use by FDs themselves, in better managing their own career and corporate contribution.

HR, personnel management and implementation

In smaller organisations, FDs may often find themselves responsible for personnel. The FD's portfolio is large enough as it is, so in this case, it would be advisable for a HR/personnel manager to report to the FD, to manage the day to day processes. These alone are a full time occupation, from recruitment, development and training, rewards and remuneration, through to industrial relations, redundancy and dismissal.

Recruitment

I have recruited many managers, up to board level. By and large, the process is still poorly managed. Some FDs are not good at this. This does not mean that they cannot become competent. Ideally FDs should have some specific recruitment experience and training and should work in tandem with the HR function, if possible. The FD would be the 'client', of course, specifying the need and the competency set and can look to the HR professional to facilitate the recruitment process. This would probably include drawing up the role description and person specification, in agreement with the FD, and recommending the medium of recruitment.

If it is found necessary to go outside to recruit, the role description and person specification are crucial. Some organisations will advertise themselves, with mixed success. Others prefer to use search and selection. As an executive recruitment consultant, I am sorry to say that organisations waste a great deal of money by not using search and selection as well as they could. Preparation is a must, before you even speak to consultants. If you are not clear what you want, they may find the wrong people.

Management and personal development

As important as taking the lead on recruitment, using the best and most appropriate skills, whether internal or external, is the need to develop and retain good people. Whether due to skills shortages, culture, a quality management philosophy or sheer economic sense, more organisations are trying to grow their own talent. The old patterns of training have changed. Leaving aside apprenticeships, or government supported schemes, organisations are increasingly tossing the responsibility for development to the individual. With the need for an increasingly flexible workforce, six month contracts are becoming the norm. This makes the individual feel less secure, but if they take a positive view, it gives them greater control of their destiny. The portfolio career has arrived. More organisations are not only offering voluntary redundancy, but are also contracting services back from their ex-employees, on an outsourced basis.

> Management has become more about managing people than managing operations; unless we have harnessed the full potential of our people even the best plans are likely to be less than entirely successful....Management development is becoming a holistic process which delivers benefit of a personal nature as well as enabling the success of the organisation....Personal development is a partnership between the individual, the organisation and the provider....In summary, we seek to create a community where an atmosphere of continual development delivers benefit to all stakeholders and to create in our people a desire to improve themselves....Life long learning is the key to both individual and corporate success. (Glyn Macken, *Professional Manager*, May 1997).

One of the ways to demonstrate a commitment to quality and people development is to undergo Investors In People accreditation. Although process driven, this has proved itself to be a mature, strategic and objective component of the organisation's overall commitment to excellence. Organisations which embark on such a programme, make a formal commitment to develop all their people in achievement of their business objectives. A training and development culture is installed, following a self-audit of the organisation's needs and skills. Both the analysis and implementation are thorough, involving everyone, before independent assessment determines whether the required standard has been achieved. Measurement against predetermined performance measures ascertains this.

Organisations which have implemented such a programme and received accreditation, have noted improvements in a wide area:

- efficiency and productivity;
- sales and customer satisfaction;
- motivation and loyalty;
- financial performance and profitability in the short and longer term.

They are proud to show off IIP accreditation alongside ISO 9000 quality standards. In the competitive world of today, anything which differentiates the organisation in the context of demonstrable quality of people and processes could augment the difference between success and failure. FDs should see these as an investment not a cost and, especially where they hold people responsibility, would do well to lead the way.

Coaching, motivation, counselling, mentoring and empowerment

> There is not a person we employ who does not, like ourselves, desire recognition, praise, gentleness, forbearance, patience. (Henry Ward Beecher).

Even if you recruit the best people, and, in partnership with the individual, develop them towards their potential, they still need to be motivated, in order to add the maximum value to delivery of the strategy. We live in highly stressful times, where many people feel insecure. It is often hardest for the most senior people in an organisation to own up to their own feelings of pressure and self-doubt, because they feel the responsibility for giving a lead. In my experience, clients who have come for counselling and personal development gain an immense release of positive energy, once they realise that someone understands and can share what is troubling them. They then find the purpose to move forward with renewed vigour. More junior people may not often have that opportunity, but they will often appreciate coaching, counselling and mentoring by senior managers with the right skills and experience.

The FD of tomorrow will need coaching, motivation, counselling and mentoring skills. The role should be just as much to create an environment where the natural talent of the team and its members can thrive, as to produce excellence in financial management. An empowering organisation can release this talent and achieve the elusive synergy of a true team. It could also be inhibited by a controlling, inflexible finance director.

> In business, people are our most important resource. Technology moves on, but people are what moves the business forward. (Sir John Harvey Jones, 1995).

While FDs may not deliver training and development themselves, they will need to have the ability:

- to set and lead the agenda;
- to determine the changing competencies which will be needed to deliver the changing requirements;
- to develop or recruit those competencies as appropriate to those requirements.

Coaching, counselling and motivating skills, especially in an environment of ongoing, 360 degree appraisal, will be fundamental.

Management and employees have different views about what is important, but also how well the organisation is performing in areas related to motivation. In a recent survey, people management was cited as the top business issue going forward into the next millennium, in four major economies of the EU. Furthermore, there was a dramatic gap between how well management perceived it was doing and what the employees thought. The three worst scores were on empowerment, job security and equality replacing status.

Mentoring is growing at such a rate that half of UK organisations, across all sectors, are using it in some form or other. A good mentor would be someone who is experienced, objective, a good listener who can be a sounding board, reflect thoughts and ideas, appropriate choices and behaviours, etc. This takes a very special set of skills, similar to those of a coach or especially a counsellor. People neither need nor want to be told what to do. They should understand and make their own choices. The mentor or counsellor skilfully creates the environment in which this can happen. If you give people advice or make choices for them, you may not only misunderstand their own personal model of the world, but also could create a dependency, from which neither the organisation, nor the individual, will gain.

Last thoughts on people

Unlike the previous edition, I have devoted much space to people management in the present text – and yet I have only scratched the surface. People are the most important, and in holistic terms the most expensive, cost to an organisation. FDs may not have traditionally come from a background where people and interpersonal skills were paramount. They are now! This does not mean that FDs cannot grow, expand, develop, acquire, or understand the necessary skills. They above all will appreciate the financial cost of people – often up to seventy-five per cent of total variable costs (not including the establishment costs to house them while they work).

13

The FD as resources manager

> Industrialism is the systematic exploitation of wasting assets...progress is merely an acceleration in the rate of that exploitation. Such prosperity as we have known up to the present is the consequence of rapidly spending the planet's irreplaceable capital. (Aldous Huxley).

To an economist there are three types of resource: land (to include all natural resources), labour, and capital.

> Choices are necessary because resources are scarce. The decision to have more of one thing necessarily implies the decision to have less of something else....Most of the problems of economics arise out of the use of resources, land, labour, and capital, to satisfy human wants. Resources are used to produce goods and services which are then consumed by households to satisfy their wants. The problem of choice arises because resources are scarce in relation to the virtually unlimited wants which they could be used to satisfy. (Lipsey, 1963).

The principle can be applied to organisations. Money may be seen by many as a resource, but even for companies it is a medium for measurement or substitution of different factors or resources. The amount available to spend is limited by the price the consumer will stand and, dependent on the profit element in that price, the amount that shareholders and lenders are prepared to put up to finance capital. The consequences are:

- first, the organisation must prioritise its use of money according to the core strategy and its other needs;

- second, it cannot afford waste;

- third, that it may need to consider substituting one factor for another (e.g. capital assets for labour);

- finally, it may need to reappraise fundamentally the way it does things (the processes), who does them and where (e.g. organisation, outsourcing, etc.)

The FD's mind, no less than anyone else's, should be open to alternatives. The ideal is that these improve quality and efficiency as well as saving costs. Merely saving costs could prove to be counterproductive.

To an organisation these resources include people and capital assets (property, machinery, transport, information systems, etc.). The FD may often lead the processes that manage many of these resources and has an obvious impact on the amount of money available to buy them. The organisation cannot afford to waste money, and one area for potential waste is taxation.

Tax

> There is no duty for taxpayers to pay more tax than that which is actually required by law because, rightly or wrongly, the Revenue or Customs believe that parliament intended something other than that which it legislated. (Peter Wyman, 1995, Chairman, ICAEW Tax Faculty).

There are four main tax types that may affect an organisation:

- corporation tax;
- VAT;
- NHI;
- capital gains tax (taxed at corporation tax rates).

In addition, operations in other countries can incur the local taxes in a country, including withholding tax. Some organisations can afford to have their own tax department or specialist, reporting to the FD. Where this is not possible, outside advisers from the external auditors, tax consultants, etc can be highly cost effective, but also provide a breadth of expertise.

Tax planning is now a complex science. It is no longer sufficient merely to calculate the tax liability and leave it at that. There are tax risks which occur from time to time, including changes of legislation. Tax planning can minimise the cost to the bottom line and help cash flow management. Some organisations have been investigated and fined for continuing old practices in relation to, PAYE for example. A multitude of business decisions can have an effect on the corporate tax or VAT position. It is possible to find ways to reduce existing bills further, for example by planning the tax or VAT consequences of capital investment decisions.

> Although at present it is the derivatives markets which are under the spotlight, equal danger of corporate loss and ultimately corporate failure exists in the area of tax risk. Sooner or later, a company which has adopted an over-aggressive structured tax saving scheme will lose a revenue challenge and find itself with a hit to the bottom line at a time when it cannot afford it. (David Timson, 1995).

Facilities management

Facilities management is a growing function of organisations, bringing together all the non-profit making or support activities under one management, sometimes under the FD. Each activity can be looked at as a profit centre or cost centre as appropriate. Each can go through a process of contracting with the business units to negotiate 'transfer' prices and agreed service standards. Some organisations have already required internal support functions to tender their services in competition with outside suppliers. This is increasingly the practice in the public sector. Such services as may be covered by facilities management might include property management, telephones, transport fleets, security, catering, waste disposal, etc.

It is not unusual for the FD to manage the property portfolio. In that case, it requires no less professional expertise than a professionally managed property fund. Maintenance is not sufficient. A large amount of dead capital can be tied up in property. Property can be volatile. Retaining a freehold rather than selling it, leasing it, or even developing it to add value is just as speculative as buying property, where prices may move either way. Returns on property will often be less than the organisation's required return on capital and the opportunity cost of property may be higher. Once again, if the organisation is not large enough to afford a professional, reporting to the FD, the advice should be contracted in or the portfolio should be contracted out.

Outsourcing

There is no part of modern business which can avoid the drive to greater efficiency, outsourcing non-core activities, buying in temporary support (at both the executive and operating levels), when permanent skills are not really needed, and leaving a much smaller core of key people who will need to be both brighter and more broadly skilled than in the past, to cope with a wider range of responsibilities. (David Timson, 1995).

For many people, facilities management has become synonymous with outsourcing. Indeed, once an organisation has gone down the FM route internally, the remaining questions are: is any of this part of our core business and if not, can any or all of it be managed outside the organisation.

Outsourcing has had a somewhat chequered history. Unfortunately, like BPR and TQM, organisations came at it from the wrong direction – cost-savings. Outsourcing is a strategic, rather than a tactical decision. If it is seen as the latter, you may get the wrong results. 'What is our core business, what do we need to focus on and can somebody else manage the non-core functions better without loss of strategic direction' are a series of strategic questions. Unfortunately, the large majority of organisations still think in a tactical rather than a strategic way.

With outsourcing, you need to be prepared to adopt the same total quality principles as if the service was still managed in-house. The key is in the contract or partnership and taking responsibility as if it was still in house. This will often be the responsibility of the FD. There needs to be a clear strategy, careful selection of partners or contractors, a detailed specification and expectations, incorporating Service Level Agreements (SLAs). It is important to realise however that it would be wrong to try and delegate strategic responsibility for IT, as it is often fundamental to the delivery of the corporate strategy and supporting the management and business processes.

A survey on outsourcing in the *Harvard Business Review*, May/June 1995, concluded that the company's overarching outsourcing objective should be to maximise flexibility and control so that it can pursue options as it learns more as its circumstances change.

For some, co-sourcing (keeping the strategy and the management but buying or contracting the necessary skills to deliver) or strategic sourcing (as e.g. Virgin PEPS fund management) may be the way forward. Outsourcing is here to stay. As the strategic pendulum swings towards virtual operation, we may instead talk of 'insourcing' as appropriate. Whatever, the FD should be critically interested, either from a financial or a strategic point of view.

Environment

The 1980s saw a surge in the public's interest in the environment. It is now an established part of most people's lives to care about what we are doing to the world we live in. There are actual costs to 'going green' but the potential benefits for organisations are less clear. There are potential costs of not caring. There are other factors at stake. If the costs have a material impact on prices this can damage competitiveness. On the other hand, public awareness of a particular company's lack of caring can damage sales and the share price.

Since 1994, accounting for the environment has moved towards the mainstream, even breaking out into accounting for sustainable resources. It is squarely in the realms of a 'stakeholder' society and company. The shareholder has a short term focus, the customer and public at large may have a longer term focus, especially where things go wrong, environmentally. As such, it becomes a market factor. The FD would be concerned at the costs of adverse publicity and damage to the brand, the costs of clean-ups. Here is where an environment policy is needed, but the FD has to balance short-term costs against longer term consequences and costs.

Among the costs that the FD should immediately be aware of are the costs of waste and energy. These and similar costs should be built in to project appraisal and lifecycle calculations. In the long term, we should be accounting for the sustainability of resources, which is both an environmental and an ethical responsibility. There may be other costs when things go wrong. It has naturally been assumed that more companies will be prosecuted as the environmental agenda tightens. What has been missed is the implicit or even explicit responsibility of individuals, who may themselves be prosecuted. This may not just be when they are knowingly and recklessly negligent or break the law. Even the MD or FD may be liable, especially where they have delegated responsibility, or they ought to have known. The directors of a company may be held liable for some of the acts of the company. This is likely to be increasingly true in the case of the environment.

As senior finance officer, the FD will gain an increasing awareness of the environment and the community within which the organisation operates. As paymaster, he or she will be called upon to fund donations and sponsorship to environment and community projects. The FD will become increasingly concerned and aware if his or her organisation is penalised by price or fine for polluting the environment. He or she will be in a position to influence company policy or strategy to minimise these potential costs. FDs will also increasingly see the value of the company playing a full role in its community and making charitable donations, rightly drawing the corporate recognition it will deserve for these initiatives. In the USA, such sponsorship has become part of corporate brand and customer perception of 'caring' organisations.

Resources and process management

Every FD needs to have some understanding of organisation, processes and systems, if only to lead others, or ask the right questions. Once an organisation or department has decided on the strategy and the way forward, the next step is to decide what resources are required to deliver the planned outcome. Fundamental to this is how to organise these resources optimally. This comes down to the people and the processes. The strategy and the business plan require a given set of competencies to deliver them. The people employed should provide that set of competencies between them. More or less than that represents inefficiency. Those people also need to be clear about what they are trying to deliver, they need to be motivated and feel empowered, as we have seen.

We have considered processes in passing, while discussing change and we shall return to the subject under quality. For the time being, any organisation needs a clearly defined set of management processes to determine how it will be managed in the process of delivering the strategy. It also needs a clearly defined and carefully designed, but flexible, set of business processes in order to achieve the practical and efficient implementation of strategy at the sharp end. All these processes need to be kept constantly under review, to determine when they need flexing or redesigning, but also to seek ways of constantly improving. Processes also need manual, mechanised, automated and computerised systems to support them.

From the FD's point of view, systems are fundamental to the provision of real-time relevant information about the qualitative and quantitative performance of the organisation. If they are not designed to support the processes, they will be costly and still fail to give all the necessary performance information.

14

The FD as information manager

The business and management processes should be no more and no less than are necessary to deliver the strategy and the business plan and will need to be capable of evolving and flexing with change. They should also fit together like a jigsaw and be in permanent dialogue with each other. The systems should be exactly what is required to support the processes, but also need to be as flexible and adaptable as possible. The information systems strategy and plan need to match and support the corporate plan and strategy.

> Modern technology facilitates the cost effective storage of large quantities of data. Today, the finance director should strive to give his company a competitive edge by developing financial information systems which transform this data into relevant information for management decisions about lines of business, products, customers and suppliers, as well as about investment projects and risk assessment. (Sir William Purves, 1995, Group Chairman, HSBC Holdings plc).

Sir William was clearly seeing a wide information systems responsibility for the FD. Indeed it is not unusual for the FD to have responsibility for the IT function alongside financial responsibilities. A wider corporate services role might also include facilities management.

Information systems are fundamental to the success of any organisation. They are fundamental to its existence. The power and availability of information processing systems mean that it is inefficient not to automate all routine tasks. Furthermore, financial and management information can be made available to the manager directly, to assist decision making. The perception is that many organisations still rely on huge, inefficient, inflexible, antiquated, main frame based processing systems. Technology has broken down most competitive barriers. The availability of information now means that what you do with it should be more important than how quickly you get it.

If any aspect of business operations and management is threatening the old fashioned FD, it is information. The new generation of staff and managers is computer literate and lives in a world of information. For leading edge organisations, information systems can genuinely differentiate from the competition. Although the lead time on new products has been reduced to months or even weeks by sophisticated technology, the real advantage lies in the quality of the processes and systems through which the organisation manages.

An enormous amount of money is still wasted in both the public and private sectors on poorly specified systems and implementation projects. Whether or not they are responsible for the function itself, FDs need to be IT literate in order to make constructive challenges. Far sighted organisations are building flexible modular systems and architectures (including the use of networks) not only to improve efficiency and competitiveness, but also with the byproduct of better cost-effectiveness. Large mainframe systems are sometimes needed, but better planning of information architectures and wider use of PCs, workstations, etc. can often achieve the same ends at less cost and with greater flexibility.

Organisations, systems and processes will need to be structured to enable efficient interchange and understanding of information. Among the challenges for the FD to consider are:

- the need for information strategy to be congruent and integral with business and organisation strategy;

- the increasing cost and changing pattern of costs of systems;

- the need to balance distribution and integration;

- the availability of systems to support key processes;

- the need for flexibility (systems cannot be set in stone);

- accuracy and reliability (fundamental to credibility); etc.

Increasingly, organisations will have to buy systems 'off the shelf' (perhaps with some modification) because tailor-made systems will be too costly, too slow to deliver and potentially too inflexible to accommodate the pace of change.

Value for money should always be under review. In order to justify the expense, benefits as well as costs should be clearly identified. Departmental budgets need to take account of:

- the costs of purchasing systems, control, integration and efficiency;

- the costs of training (these can multiply if there is no corporate IT purchasing standard, as people buy different software from different suppliers, requiring different training and support needs);

- support costs, which can typically be up to twenty per cent oncost; etc.

One of the worst examples which is frequently encountered is the proliferation of different word processing, spreadsheet, database and other office packages within the same organisation.

Apart from the falling costs of information, the good news is that different systems will be better able to receive and translate data exchanged between each other, as manufacturers allow emulation between each other's products and international standards converge. Furthermore, object orientation and other techniques will allow users more flexibility and control in the use and evolution of their information systems.

Information strategy and the board

> Companies which complain that IT isn't meeting their needs must bear some responsibility for this failure. Often they have no coherent IT strategy and take a narrow view of its uses....For the vast majority of companies, computers at best automate yesterday's manual systems, at worst leave them wallowing in a morass of ill-matched boxes that are apparently incapable of yielding useful information. Small wonder so many organisations are slashing their IT budgets and subcontracting their entire computer operations to third parties. (Jane Bird, 'The Trouble with IT', November 1994, *Management Today*).

Whether or not the FD is directly responsible for IT/IS at a corporate level, he or she needs to understand the principles and management for his or her own department and is also a key player in the executive team which determines them and drives them at the corporate level. The costs of shortfall will be measured in terms of money, quality, speed of response and competitiveness. The FD is also a key member of the board which determines and monitors the delivery of the overall strategy.

There is no doubt that IT should be represented at board level. It would be simple to justify this on the basis of business dependence on technology for delivery. IT strategy needs representation. Implementation is being more routinely outsourced, e.g. to the Indian subcontinent. IT strategy is fundamental to corporate strategy simply because information management (or more generally knowledge management) has already become a key differentiator for the 21st century. What counts now is how we capture and use knowledge to competitive advantage.

The consequences for the FD are many, but particularly:

- increasingly, the FD is responsible for IT, on the basis of shortage of IT directors and the assigned importance of financial management information systems;

- second, because apart from fundamentally changing the way the enterprise is organised, IT/IS have material financial consequences, not just in the cost of the latter, but in the financial consequences of changing the way in which people work;

- third, whether or how the FD will obtain the knowledge and understanding to capitalise on these fundamental strategic considerations;

- finally, the raft of immediate challenges, but specifically year 2000, EMU and the growth of real-time reporting and the virtual, global corporation.

There might be a need for an IT expert on board, but you have to get the right person. People who are purely focused on technology are often unable to grasp the business issues. At present, IT is falling down in areas such as manufacturing and resource planning. The solution may be to encourage operational directors to take charge of IT at board level. (John Acornley, 1996, FD of Baxi Group).

This is a far-sighted FD, but knowledge management goes way beyond the IT systems which support the key processes of the organisation. Knowledge is in the prime capital of the business – the people – and is often captured in the processes by which the organisation delivers its strategy. It may or may not be stored in the information systems. It is of immeasurable and growing value to all organisations, viz the disparity between the asset value and market capitalisation of high-tech companies. Therefore, its strategic importance is much greater than IT/IS. This may be the biggest challenge of all to the FD.

In practical terms there are immediate difficulties for the FD who leads IT. FDs do not always understand IT and IT specialists do not always understand finance or even business. We have allowed, tolerated, even encouraged the growth of technical IT functions, justifying delegation on the basis of not being able to understand the language and jargon of IT. We do understand the costs of IT and IS, however, especially when things go wrong. There is a shortage of specialist skills in the market place, even for day to day needs, let alone year 2000, EMU and other pressing needs. We have allowed a culture to develop training business and finance managers inadequately in IT understanding.

New opportunities

Leaving aside year 2000 for a moment, there is an exciting different future for all, especially the FD, in which virtual companies can be started from scratch and grown to astonishing proportions in a short time; a future where large scale need no longer be an advantage. Take financial services. While we are seeing the growth of the global mega-players, by rationalisation and merger, we are also seeing weekly the start-up of new niche businesses, e.g. Boots, Shell and Kwik-Fit selling financial services.

The opportunity, development and growth of these businesses is possible because we live in an age of knowledge management. If you buy the knowledge to set up and run such businesses, the technology already exists to support them (or you can outsource, or buy in all the necessary functions). This is the age of value-added; both real and perceived. Real, in the sense that if there is sufficient margin, other players can move in. Perceived, in the sense that brands are being created and transported to all manner of often unrelated products. Virgin started by selling records. It now sells transport, financial services, and so on.

So, we live in the age of knowledge management and intellectual capital. Simply look at the growth of IPR, in the sense of how much is being captured, legally protected and sold globally. Expert systems have been around for some time. Now they have grown up and the greatest growth medium for the next century will be the Internet. This is now effectively a living, thinking organism.

We are already going beyond the knowledge era to the thinking era. Supercomputers and computer clusters can already operate as superintelligent and thinking machines. They cannot go beyond the power of the human brain yet, but they are learning fast, in a more purposeful way. Supercomputers already understand more about the human genome than any one human. It will be totally decoded before the turn of the century. Humans have the neurology to store, process and understand as well and as fast as supercomputers (together with the USP of feelings and emotions), but our brains have not been trained. Link them together through the Internet and get them in communication and you have a thinking potential which computing power will never match. Companies like 3M already have such corporate brains. fifteen per cent of time is thinking time and twenty-five per cent of all income must come from products introduced in the previous four years.

Global, virtual operation

In early 1998, Unisys had already set up a series of 'virtual factories' throughout the world, to enable any organisation running on a selection of computer languages to check and update their code for year 2000 compatibility. Some say this problem will hit us on 9.9.99. Who knows how many viruses will be timed to go off on that date, 1.1.00, or even 01.01.01. For many it has already arrived. Credit cards have already been refused with expiry dates beyond 2000 and lawsuits pursued, where goods have been rejected because their sell-by date is beyond 2000.

While we already live in a world of global operation, this does not mean the death knell for smaller enterprises. Indeed, the FD or MD who is canny and takes the time to understand how IT and IS can make the difference, may score just as heavily as the manufacturer with a new product. The difference is in knowledge, how to pool it, how to use it. The need is for the FD to understand the value of knowledge and intellectual capital, protect it, secure it and exploit it, aided by the virtual systems capability which already exists. The Internet is mainstream, the virtual world is now. We already have intranets being created and these are supporting creative strategic alliances, which will be the basis of stakeholder enterprises.

There are many strategic challenges for government and organisations. It is the FD who should have the holistic awareness and the financial understanding to ask the informed questions which lead to added value and efficiency, rather than cost-cutting and perpetuation of outdated processes and systems. The trouble is that there is too much vested interest in the latter. If, through knowledge databases, inter and intra nets, the knowledge in individuals can be captured, there is the potential for huge corporate gain. Small companies could grow at an extraordinary rate if they grasp this opportunity, create a virtual technology base and exploit the knowledge for competitive advantage. Only one of the ways is through design and continuous improvement of the processes.

The virtual company will not be structured as before. It will be based on a tight core and a set of flexing and adapting strategic alliances between stakeholders, some of whom might have been employees. The company will be supported by on-line, real-time reporting and management information systems. Where any physical movement is involved, one of the skills in greatest demand will be systems based logistics. Discussions about cost-cutting or economies of scale could be made irrelevant if the corporation is created or redesigned around a global network of strategic alliances, infinitely flexible to stakeholders' needs. Reworking a raw material into a product can only add finite value, until originality and uniqueness of design, brand and knowledge are added. The latter can create limitless opportunity.

Practical consequences

Among the practical consequences of this brave new world for the FD will be stakeholder reporting, real-time online reporting and auditing of the global business. Accounting and auditing standards will have to become global, if only to cope with the demands of the Internet. Auditors should already be signing off statements on the Internet. The value-adding digital economy will be based on expert systems and information engineering. Low-level work will be automated, or outsourced from regions of the globe where low cost labour can still be exploited. In the western economies, specialisation will grow at an exponential rate, while software replaces the general and the routine.

The implementation challenges lie primarily in the fact that business management and use of IT are not working well. This is largely due to ignorance both ways. Technology development should now be driven by business objectives and need in society. The balance changed from hardware constraints to software long ago, when the chip became so cheap that technology solutions could be made available in weeks rather than years. The alert in the IT industry moved to being business solutions driven, rather than hardware constrained. The Internet takes this process further. Unisys will solve year 2000 problems down the line to their virtual factories, while the fastest growing software supplier will install systems down the line, rather than through floppy disk or CD ROM. Both will save industry a fortune.

The failure of new systems still largely results from an inability to define the need and the business requirements. This is as true of financial information systems as any other. Especially in this area, organisations should have moved long ago from buying bespoke systems to packaged suites, adapting their own internal processes to fit. Information is time stamped and historical by nature. Even the most sophisticated system can deliver worthless information if it is too late. It is long overdue for users to own their own systems, whether management, production or financial information. Abdication to the IT director or the FD can lead to unusable irrelevant information, repudiated by people at the sharp end. The precision of the data is less important than what you do with it. The result is the growth of a hybrid business role in the business information analyst placed between the user, or FD, and the IT specialist.

Who manages all this is irrelevant. They should report at board level. They should be able to think holistically in order to anticipate the needs of all parties and stakeholders, and the IS/IT systems and processes themselves could be totally outsourced. In the virtual company they may never be insourced in the first place.

Changing ways of working – service, unbundling and outsourcing

The changing role of the FD will increasingly reflect changing patterns of industry and ways of working and managing. Because of potential economies and cost efficiencies, the FD will be in the van of many of these developments. One way to influence the organisation's cost efficiency is for the FD to implement these new ways of working in the finance function and IT first.

> All firms are becoming professional service firms....Value-added in the economy
> – and for the corporation – will come from knowledge....all economic organisation
> is fast becoming an almost pure knowledge play. Today seventy-five to ninety-five
> per cent of a typical manufacturer's payroll is 'service sector'/knowledge
> employees – information systems experts, designers, engineers, accountants,
> marketers, trainers. (Peters, 1993).

Finance is no longer in control of the organisation. Finance is a professional service firm. There is no part of the function which could not be theoretically provided by another service organisation. The finance function is also potentially a fixed cost – an overhead, needing to sell itself to the organisation. This does not mean that the governance, strategic, advisory, etc. functions of the FD will be contracted out, but as teams and parts of the organisation become more self-sufficient, they will want value for money if they buy the services of the finance function. Many of these financial services can be bought outside from a growing number of service providers. There will also be the possibility of the finance function selling these services elsewhere to obtain or take advantage of economies of scale. As with the rest of the organisation, the FD should look at what is core in the finance function and determine the best and most cost-effective way to deliver those services. If the IT function can be outsourced, so can finance.

Whatever the pattern of delivery, the information necessary to manage the business will be distributed through networks to where it is needed. It will be consolidated and integrated at the centre only for the purposes of overall reporting, while flexible systems take the strain. The role of the accountants has changed, from one of number crunching and month-ends, to supporting and advising the business. Provided managers can see their unit information before anyone else (and ideally real time), this will not present a threat. The client/server concept will not be confined to the IT architecture, it will be the way the service is delivered, from wherever. 'A major drive behind client/server has been the demand, from major corporations, for business critical data to be at the fingertips of those who need it: the decision makers.' (Lesley Meall, November 1994, *Accountancy*).

Implementation of information systems

Where the FD has responsibility for IT also, the arguments sharpen further. So many management information systems have become standardised and modularised, that one wonders how the cost of tailoring everything can be justified, especially taking account of delivery times and, especially where specification has been inaccurate or incomplete, the occasional inappropriateness of the solutions. There is still a slavish adherence to the god of bespoking in many IT departments, with in-house people still writing their own solutions. While modularised systems supplied by the likes of Oracle may be seen as a sledgehammer to crack a nut, they offer speed, economy and flexibility by tailoring the front end or parts of the solution, rather than writing from scratch. The latter requires the user to freeze their needs far too early in the timescale. Users often do not take proper ownership of the solution, howl when it does not deliver and suffer when they have to go to the back of the queue for revisions and modifications. Why would the FD want to stand in line for criticism, by virtue of heading up IT, when applying a broader, rational view can satisfy the user and the FD?

The cost of IT is a major issue, despite the advent of the PC and the move from monolithic central systems to distributed networked systems. Is this an illusion, or sleight of hand? IT costs in total are now second after people costs. Why is this? There are three main reasons:

- the 'hidden' costs;
- poor financial and inefficient business management (as touched on above);
- the advent of the PC.

Costs have grown disproportionately, despite outsourcing of hardware and software and falling costs of the technology. The main reason, despite falling unit costs and exploding capacity and power of the PCs themselves, is the maintenance, software update and training costs, many of which are now localised, rather than centralised. The PC was originally designed as a stand-alone, miniaturised, hardware option. Now we have networked them and the software options have exploded. Without a central buying strategy for the hardware and software, different brands will proliferate and diseconomies grow.

I have never known an IT solution of any significant size which delivered a financial return on investment. They are rather like freezers, they simply improve the quality of your consumption (in this case, of information). Even where the FD is in charge of IT, there is often a communication and understanding gap between the technical and finance staff. Whereas business managers think in terms of global markets and customer satisfaction, IT experts think in terms of hardware platforms and software solutions. With the rate of technological change, there is no waiting to get on the merry-go-round. I have known many IT departments which bought the latest gizmo or software package on the grounds of consumer testing. Even where solutions deliver the information, they may not give return on investment. Like the FD, the IT manager should be a facilitator of solutions which meet and flex with the customer need.

If there is one area where FDs and MDs may not have the experience or understanding to ask the right questions, it is IT. Is this a surprise? Not if you reflect on a February 1998 MORI survey for *Management Today*. From this: one quarter of top managers had no PC in the office or at home; one quarter of FDs were responsible for IT; and two thirds of organisations claimed to have an IT strategy committee, usually chaired by the FD. Why? Because IT is seen as a cost, where it is poorly understood. The CEO should lead the way in using IT, making it a priority to understand and using system delivered information to ask the question. With so many FDs responsible for IT, all should be asking why it does not deliver a return on investment.

Costs

In the office, the cost of the hardware is estimated at only one fifth of total IT costs. One needs to add in:

- the cost of management time, to specify needs, install, sort them out and then apply them to the systems;
- warranties, maintenance, technical support, training and software licences;
- consumables;
- security and insurance costs.

There are two ways of minimising costs; buying off the shelf; and financing alternatives.

Now that software is the driver, the position is less clear, but markets have become more flexible. Hardware and solutions can still be leased, often by the supplier, sometimes in the high street. For software, this is less often true, but two important areas for consideration are bulk licences and year 2000/EMU solutions. In the former case, borrowing, spreading the payments through the supplier, or even renting the software over a network may prove to be the best longer term solutions. In the matter of the year 2000 and EMU problems, many organisations may neither be able to afford nor justify the costs of modification. It would be easier to justify buying completely new year 2000 and EMU compliant systems to last for the next few years and probably easier to obtain finance also.

Apart from the costs of the IT/IS resources, there is also the matter of people costs. The scarcity of specialists, especially in the run-up to 2000, is a strong argument in favour of outsourcing as much as you can. The best investment will be in your business managers, in understanding the technology, how to specify it and how to use it to competitive advantage, rather than rafts of expensive technicians. For the FD it still comes back to the need to understand the holistic business, the need to see everyone as a customer, the need to understand enough about information systems to ask the right questions, especially if they double up IT responsibility. Wearing the FD hat, the governance hat, or the IT hat, the FD cannot avoid responsibility for year 2000 and EMU.

As head of IT, the FD will want to look at the best way to implement systems to deliver the information management needs to make informed decisions, especially financial information, but also at the most economical way of providing such information. IT strategy in the past seemed to be about two main things, buying the right hardware to store and process the data and writing or buying the right software to convert that data into usable information. For reasons discussed earlier, the IT department was sometimes the tail wagging the dog and management conspired in this by allowing IT to become highly technical, as opposed to business oriented, while business managers took insufficient time and trouble to demystify IT and bend it to their own purposes. Business should be driven by the needs of the customer and so should IT.

In terms, therefore, of how management information systems will be implemented and supported, the discussion must centre around information collected in data warehouses, or through relational databases, distributed through the Internet or intranets, 'mined', managed and represented by flexible combinations of software, accessed down the line. This will apply to the periodic and annual accounting and reporting of financial and business performance, along the lines discussed earlier. SMEs may say that this vision is beyond them, now or in the future. It is here now, so plan for it. Without it you will lose competitive advantage, you will not support a stakeholder enterprise and your role will remain closer to the abacus than the holistic, strategic FD of tomorrow.

The Internet

In this section, I can only hope to alert, inform and excite about the possibilities that developing IT and the Net can offer the FD to improve economy and efficiency. It is for the user to tailor their own needs and develop the competitive advantage. For the SME, there are particular advantages as information processing and knowledge engineering become more accessible and affordable. The Internet began as a marketing, information and e-mail medium. Now it is a base for worldwide business applications and electronic commerce, currently on an unregulated global basis with the risks and concerns that brings. It has become a process for disintermediation, bringing closer contact with customers and suppliers and affording the basis of the virtual corporation, in reality rather than science fiction. Thousands of such companies already exist.

Even before most organisations have come to terms with the Net, we have the extraordinary growth of intranets. These are closed subsets of the Internet, supported and communicating through the worldwide web, providing internal communications media within organisations, or even between them and their stakeholders. Through these, ideas and information can be shared, exchanged, discussed and evolved, rapidly. For the FD, there is already the opportunity to publish a range of company information, including financial and management reports, sales information and even internal telephone directories. Indeed, 3M, Hewlett Packard and others have the equivalent of internal Yellow Pages capturing who is thinking about or working on what and where.

Intranets and, indeed the Internet itself, save transport and meeting costs, leased lines, time (including the interminable problem of diary matching), etc. They serve a growing army of people with the choice of home working, 'hot desking' or fixed location offices. They will also enable the FD to go out to the internal customer – real time, virtual in cyberspace.

Financial information systems

While much of the foregoing redefines the concept of financial information systems, there remain for the time being software packages of high sophistication and immense power, which have made understanding the financial performance more affordable. Many FDs may feel they have little or no choice in accounting or financial reporting, struggling on with outdated, inflexible systems, still often DOS based, producing paper, or reporting through old-fashioned terminals.

It need not be that way. We are approaching a watershed. The catalyst will be the millennium. Most accounting systems and/or feeder systems for financial and business performance are still not year 2000 compliant. Given that computer projects always overrun, it is already too late to modify most of those systems. It is certainly too late to start. For many, the only rational choice is to start again. In IT especially, every such problem can be an opportunity.

Financial information systems are often, in the words of a former IT director, like spaghetti. It is true that sophisticated modern analytical, relating and integrating tools can help to divine sense out of apparent nonsense, but it might be better to start again. For many organisations, the need to account predated the need to report holistic business performance. Systems were knitted together to provide the necessary information. While search software and browsers can find their way through the audit trail of information, it must be better to structure it the way management needs it now.

It makes sense to start with the strategy, design the management and business processes to implement that strategy, determine the micro and macro measures of performance and structure the systems accordingly. Now may be too late for some to start, but the availability of rational decision support systems, analytical tools, search engines, financial information packages, data warehouse and RDBMS systems and front-end Windows based presentation packages offer so much more flexibility for the FD of the future. If FDs are responsible for IT, the way forward is to understand and meet customers' information needs and deliver them, not to present them with unintelligible, outdated information.

Year 2000

The second edition of this book was typed using an old copy of Microsoft Word, on a DX/75 laptop. Nowadays, I use it only as a word processor. On 31 December 1999, it will be redundant and retired, like any FD who reads this and still has not woken up to the year 2000 problem. In this section, I could also write about EMU, but that is reserved for elsewhere. Suffice to say that, if you are not one of those who know you will be year 2000 compliant by 1 January 2000, or one of those with completely new systems that will cope with both, forget about EMU. Year 2000 will wipe you out.

On Breakfast TV on 26 March 1998, Robin Guenier, Head of Taskforce 2000 said 'if you haven't started, you are already too late.' In 1995, alerted by a local businessman, David Atkinson MP asked an oral question of the then prime minister, following several written questions to government departments. The question was treated with ridicule. Since then, the only obvious public commitment of any significance was the establishment of Taskforce 2000 and 'Bug Busters'. Why, because government already knew that it could not make its own systems totally compliant by that date.

What is year 2000, or the Millennium Timebomb? For convenience and to save space in file structures, the year code on many computer programs was abbreviated to two digits. When the century turns, 99 will click over to 00, but computers will not know whether it is 2000 or 1900. Computers will either thrash around endlessly, or stop. Systems will crash. Even the clever and foresighted companies which are already compliant, may be brought down by their suppliers or business partners. Lawsuits are underway. Chips, software and hardware are still being sold which are not compliant. Microchips are installed in every electronically controlled device we take for granted, from clocks and cars to life support systems. Nobody knows everything which will fail, because where investment is being made, it is in making manufacturers and businesses compliant, not the products.

The worldwide cost has been estimated at $2 trillion, for compliance and consequential work alone. The cost to the world economy and society is incalculable.

The world as we know it may end at midnight on 31 January 1999, but a different world will emerge in the years that follow. For those companies that survive, the rewards could be limitless. Countless products will literally be scrap overnight. Apart from the chance of selling huge amounts of new products and services, there will also be the opportunity to redesign completely products and computer systems, resulting in a paradigm shift, once the dust has died down. The major economies of the world may suffer the greatest costs, but the lesser economies have hardly started to worry about the problem, let alone address it. This could truly be a time when the rich get richer at the expense of the poor.

Some time between now and then, there will be a major setback in the world stock markets. Traders are already hedging the risks. There will then be a multi-stage adjustment. After the first major shock, an element of disbelief will develop and a feeling that the falls have been overdone. This will be followed by a deeper setback. As hard evidence emerges about which companies are compliant, there will be differential recovery in their shares. A later setback will occur as the effects of suppliers and other infrastructure factors on some of those companies suggest further losses or failures. In the months following the date change, as evidence grows that some companies have survived, their stocks will surge dramatically, due to demand factors. If you want your money safe, invest in UK Government Securities. They already have 2000+ maturity dates, and the UK is less badly placed than anywhere except the US. However, be prepared for more stock to be issued, to pay for the government's own one-off costs.

Is this Doomsday? You bet! It is calculated to make the reader think of nothing else and after they have followed the steps outlined later, successfully I hope, start worrying about EMU and then corporate debt. If you think you can escape all but the personal consequences of the unrest in early 2000, go now, but even now you may not escape personal liability for the financial consequences if your company fails. The media has been littered with warnings for two years. No professional magazine has missed a reference to the growing crisis in any issue in the last year. In 1998, we will see the first of a flood of audit qualifications, on the grounds that the company's viability is at risk, or already doomed. The rate of corporate failure in the three years beginning in January 1999 will be unparalleled in history. Each one carries the incremental risk that other sound, well-prepared companies will be brought down in their wake, through lack of supply or vital support services. For many of you, FDs and other readers, the rest of this section may be of academic interest. I hope so. You are either not working, or your business is fireproof (a market stall maybe?).

There may be a few organisations which, having not started the process yet, will still survive. While many businesses under £10 million will be at risk, depending on the degree of sophistication and the costs they are prepared to stand, they may be able to replace all their systems and start again. Anyone accounting manually will have an advantage, except that most money comes through payment systems these days and these may fail, or may not be secure. One of the problems which no-one has mentioned is the certainty that virus creators will have targeted 00.01.01.01.00 as the magic date to launch their latest and most devastating creations. Many of these will be year 2000 compliant. Then there are the hackers, who could create mayhem in early 2000, when many computer systems will be like shopfronts after a bomb blast. How many people will have overlooked their virus protection? Virus writers and hackers are much cuter than FDs and business managers. They ply their trade by always being ahead of the game.

For those of you who are still reading, what might you be able to do? First, revise your estimates of the likely cost upwards. If you are going to publish a profits alert at some stage, work out the worst case value in conjunction with your auditors. The most likely estimate will be far too low. IT projects always overrun, in time and cost. The cost of resources to sort matters out will rocket over the next year, until it becomes prohibitive or it is too late to act. The first practical step, if you have not already taken it (like an alarming number of organisations) is a compliance audit. If you trade or buy in European markets, factor in the cost of Euro accounting as well. You will need to be EMU compliant long before the UK joins up. A word of warning, however. Unless you are acquiring completely new systems, do not attempt to make both sets of changes at the same time. The experts consider this to be too risky.

The basic options are to rewrite, replace or wind up the business while you have positive net worth. You could always start again in two years time! If you are still in the game, cancel all non-priority systems work and then cancel everything else. The estimated resource needed to sort out the total problem is greater than the total UK IT industry. If you end up with spare resource, you could contract it at a handsome rate to other companies. That is, if your own people are not lured away by promises of £500 a day, rising well above that before the end of the century.

Check all your hardware and software, especially PCs and their applications. Both are still being sold without year 2000 compliance! Before you scrap your PCs, check on the possibility of replacing the chip, and upgrading to the fastest Pentium at the same time. Other parts may have to go, you may need to replace and reload all or much of your software and rebuild many of your files, from hardcopy. Meanwhile, think of all the accumulated rubbish you can dump. For larger machines and more complex software and files, the solution is not that easy. Some proprietary solutions are already on sale. Most of them will simply buy you the time to sort out the problem after 2000, when resource starts to become available.

Where will you get the resources to carry out the revisions? It is probably too late, but apart from reactivating existing staff or retired staff with the appropriate skills, you could consider training or retraining existing staff or new entrants. Alternatively, like many others you could export the problem to other countries, e.g. India, or the Unisys 'virtual factories'. Assuming you manage to sort out all your own problems, you should also be checking your suppliers and customers now. In the meantime, you might need a plan.

The need for a plan

First, create a task force, probably headed by the FD, whose breadth of training and responsibility will be valuable. Seek advice from auditors, IT suppliers and software associations and user groups. Check all your software and hardware. Do not overlook the need to check interfaces – internal and external. They can bring down totally compliant systems. Having cancelled all other priorities, start with the most critical and problematic of the systems. Do not be afraid to scrap and start again, if that is a viable option. You will not have that option if you defer doing this until later. It takes time to specify, install and test systems, especially where they interface with others. Create a contingency plan wherever possible for using manual systems to tide you over.

The entire information systems should be checked and tested for year 2000 compliance, including live data. Change the dates on a test run and see what happens. This is what MP David Atkinson did on his own laptop in 1995. When he switched it back on it showed January 1980! Then he realised the seriousness of the problem. Run the systems pre and post the date change and compare the data meticulously. You won't get a second chance. However you have implemented the changes, through new systems or revisions, run them again, tested and updated, throughout 1999. Check that everyone else you engage with is year 2000 compliant. BT has warned it will cancel all contracts with partners who are not, well before the date. Demand a year 2000 warranty from everyone who claims to be complaint, if necessary certified by a third party. In 1998 we shall see many company accounts qualified for non-compliance. Check especially anyone to whom you are connected for business purposes.

The bonus could be that you dramatically improve the efficiency of your existing processes and systems, even if you do become compliant. In the meantime, issue a formal company policy that anyone connecting unauthorised hardware or introducing unauthorised software onto company systems will face immediate dismissal. This would not seem draconian if non-compliant hardware, software or a real Millennium bug (i.e. virus) wiped you out after all the hard work.

If you are still feeling confident, reflect on these few facts. Lawsuits have already been filed for year 2000 non-compliance. Bank and credit cards have already been rejected because they have a 2000 expiry date. If you are aware of a problem now, or could be deemed to be, failure in 2000 may lead to litigation against you personally by those who lose out, including class actions by shareholders or customers. Insurance against this risk is impossible or prohibitive. EMU awaits. Europe is behind the UK for year 2000. All the leading economies besides the UK are trying to do both in two years! Many other overseas countries either remain blissfully unaware of the problem (like more than fifty per cent of companies in the UK) or have already given up trying to do anything about it. Meanwhile, a real practical worry is in the financial risks related to payment systems, UK and overseas banks, customers payments and the stock markets of the world. If panic sets in, financial institutions may see a run on them.

That is enough on year 2000. The subject will be academic for one reason or another in 2000. For some it has already become academic – but do they realise?

Security

The subject of systems security may seem mundane following the previous section. The FD needs to be aware of the major risks, both as FD and as auditor. Physical security has become harder to achieve, due to the miniaturisation of systems since the advent of the PC and the widespread distribution of hardware as 'office furniture'. There are many proprietary physical devices available, but the theft of a computer is relatively insignificant when compared to the security of the systems themselves. Any number of virus protection products are available, but like the common thief, the writers of viruses manage to stay ahead of the game. Fire and water damage can also bring an organisation's systems to a halt.

In my experience, if an organisation cannot account at all for three days, it is likely to fail. Apart from security devices, regularly backing up data is a must, however inconvenient. I lost my entire hard disc while writing this second edition. It took two days to reinstall all the software, but I was able to restore my data files from back up tape in ten minutes. I then had the bonus of clearing out a lot of rubbish I had accumulated.

As the Pentagon has experienced, you can never keep out a determined hacker. Some are malicious, some are criminals and some are playing a game or trying to prove a point. Visible organisations attract more attention. Connection to the Internet has transformed business and personal life and it will grow at a phenomenal rate in the next few years. It brings with it new security risks, both in terms of viruses and hackers. Businesses have also been brought down by rogue organisers and even competitors blitzing companies with faxes and e-mails and overloading their systems. Apart from risks such as these, spoof web sites, industrial espionage, electronic theft, etc., there is a real concern that there is no regulatory framework or code of security practice for this 'global property'.

The devices to protect your business do not come cheap: electronic tunnels (to prevent unauthorised access to a communication), firewalls and electronic gates that check for certain security devices before admitting entry, scramblers which encrypt data, Secure Electronic Transactions (SETs) to secure payments, etc. Consumers are still unsure about the risks, but e-commerce is growing at an astonishing rate, despite it not originally being built for that purpose. For the FD, the balance of probabilities is favourable when considering not only the global, commercial opportunities (at the price of a local call), but also the potential for more sophisticated financial and business information systems, using the Internet and especially intranets (or even extranets).

15

The FD as relationship manager

> Cooperation is not so much learning how to get along with others as taking the kinks out of yourself so that others can get along with you. (Ian Ferguson).

The FD cannot afford to be passive about any of the many relationships for which he or she has the leading responsibility. Any of them can have financial consequences, for good or ill. In the old days, managers would focus attention on the relationships with customers. These days, it is almost as important to be a good (internal) customer. As a customer you can gain valuable experiences which can enrich your role as a supplier. If you are treated badly as a customer, reflect for a moment whether any of your people or even you may exhibit the same traits in the way you deal with your own customers.

Shareholders or stakeholders?

> A key aspect of the FD's role is 'playing a major part in relations with actual and potential investors in the company, in both equity and debt markets. The finance director is key to those markets having confidence in the company, whether or not they are current investors.' (Chief Executive, 1995, electricity company).

> Another source of pressure, especially for large companies, is the growing emphasis on external communications. While the importance of investor relations is not new, large institutions are probing more deeply into the companies in which they hold substantial stakes. The finance director is closely involved in maintaining these relationships. (Sir Geoffrey Owen, 1995).

This preoccupation with looking after shareholders first is a potentially narrow focus. There is no doubt of the need to look after all key relationships diligently. What some enlightened companies have discovered however is that if you have a preoccupation with quality and your customers, the results can be reflected in above average customer loyalty and consequent performance, with consequent benefits for the shareholder. The balance is changing.

Every organisation has stakeholders. As well as shareholders and customers, there are others, including suppliers. In the public sector, stakeholders would include, for example, the government, electors, taxpayers, purchasers of healthcare in the NHS, patients, ratepayers, schoolchildren and parents. No organisation in this day and age can afford not to be aware of, listen to and encourage participation from its stakeholders of all kinds.

Managing investor relations

To dwell for a moment on shareholders, bankers and financiers, however, these relationships can of course be critical. It has been shown in the USA, for example, that where customers feel they get particularly good service, they are not only more likely to maintain a longer term relationship with the supplier, but are also often prepared to pay a premium price. Part of the job of the corporate FD is to help ensure long term growth of shareholder value. Where companies place high value on this relationship and demonstrate it, not only through consistent performance, but also through the way they deal and communicate with shareholders (and, for example, shareholder incentives) their shares can show above average performance.

> The science of investor relations seems to have changed over the last few years. The rules change periodically and the techniques become forever more sophisticated. However, at the end of the day, it is probably no more sophisticated than a salesman's diary system. It is just that it feels more complicated. (R N Chisman, 1995, FD, Stakis plc).

The key players in developing and sustaining investor relations are the chairman, managing director and finance director. Two or three representatives of these will be found in at least one broadsheet newspaper every day, presenting the results of yet another company. Not only presentation of the annual and interim results, but also shareholder and analyst meetings can make a great deal of difference in how the shares of a company perform and are valued. Nowadays, the share registers of most companies are dominated by institutional shareholders. Time spent visiting them or the sector analysts can reap rewards for the enlightened company. The FD would often be expected to lead this process and managing shareholder relationships will appear in many job descriptions.

In any investor relations programme responsibilities must be clear cut. Again, at GKN I will lead with the institutional shareholders and the media, with the help of the director of corporate affairs, and the finance director will lead with the broker's analysts. But it is also important to introduce your shareholders to other members of your executive team. At all our major investor relations meetings we will have, in addition to the chief executive and finance director, at least one other executive director. (Sir David Lees, 1995, Chairman and Chief Executive of GKN).

Media and communication

The media can be a friend or an enemy. Profit warnings provide an excellent example. Although FDs may become increasingly frustrated at trying to balance the company's long term plans and aspirations against the market's 'short termism', the FD should cultivate relationships with the sensible media, especially those who appear favourably disposed to the company. This includes not only being accessible, but also going out of one's way to provide early information or warnings (though not of course before the issue of a public statement).

It is critically important for any company to manage its relationships with the media. You should not be caught off guard. When bad news breaks, especially when it is known about, as in profit warnings, you cannot afford to be unavailable. 'No comment' is not a good response, unless you are asked a question which you are unable to answer, such as commenting on as yet unpublished results, or making forecasts. A press conference may not always be appropriate or may represent overkill, but the FD should make time to brief favourable journalists or at least be available for comment, where there is news on which to comment. A prepared brief or a promise to return the call with a considered response is much preferable.

Profit warnings may appear to some to have become the bane of quoted companies' lives. There are, of course, circumstances where changed conditions produce an unplanned shortfall, such as a sharp change in the value of the currency over a short period. In other situations, the effect on the share price may reflect not only a rerating of the company, but also a comment on the competence of management (especially the FD). While they should be avoided if possible, through awareness and forward planning, the Yellow Book of the Stock Exchange states that they are mandatory when the directors become aware 'that there is such a change in the company's financial condition or in the performance of its business or in the company's expectation of its performance that knowledge of the change is likely to lead to a substantial movement in the price of its listed securities'. Of course, it is common for a profit warning to produce at least as big a change in itself.

In terms of general guidance, the watchword is 'no surprises'. Where an adverse position does arise, the first thing to do is determine exactly what the problem is and make an early, considered response. The most important thing is to make sure that the world believes management is in control and doing a competent job. As in any business setback, by the time the information is announced, management should already know what it is doing about it (or has already done about it). Being available and considering the impact on all stakeholders are especially important, including in the public sector.

> Time spent on communication, though at times burdensome, is not time wasted – rather the reverse. If you operate an investor relations programme well the result will be that your shareholders have a better understanding of the business and the drivers of the business. That's to everyone's advantage. (Sir David Lees, 1995).

The annual report

Another area which has seen substantial improvement and cannot be underestimated is that of the annual report, even in the public sector. Many FDs still see the annual accounts as so much grey matter, alleviated occasionally by bits of artwork or library photos. What they overlook is that for many organisations, the annual report is the only satisfactory medium for the outside world to get anywhere near what is really happening in the organisation. While many would not wish to be too ostentatious, we are not talking just about creating a corporate image. It has become expected that the strategy, culture, vision, values, goals, environment and community policies will be communicated through this medium. For companies in competitive markets, it is another means to develop the brand perception. The directors, facilitated by the FD, should be clear on what they do want to say, not what they do not want to say.

There is a misguided belief that you can give away competitive advantage by being too open, but people trust customer relationships with more open organisations, especially where the message is clear and consistent. After all, so much boardroom, executive and management effort is devoted to the agreement and production of the annual report that the company might as well derive some lasting value from the expense. As an afterthought, it is only a matter of time before organisations in all sectors produce their annual report on the Net, as well as in print, on the way to 'real time' reporting in the 21st century.

Suppliers

It has been suggested earlier that relationships with suppliers are as important in their own way as those with customers. They can pay dividends in terms of speed and quality of service. Payment of suppliers is a tricky issue, however. It would be easy to say that suppliers should always be paid on the agreed terms of business. Much resentment and even financial difficulty has been attributed to, for example, large companies who stretch their suppliers' patience by exceeding the agreed terms for payment. Some companies have even been forced out of business.

Management of cash flow is critical to a company's survival. Lack of cash causes more company failures than lack of capital (although the latter can of course contribute to the former). In managing the working capital requirements of a company, it is easy to see that delaying creditor payments and chasing debtors can have a dramatic effect on cash flow and even investment earnings. The debate will not go away and representations have even been made to government to intervene. There is, however, no doubt that if you go out of your way to look after your suppliers and pay them on time, you will tend to get better service than the company which does not. You may only find out the consequences of not doing so when a crisis occurs, when you need a favour, or when you introduce 'just in time' methods to your operations.

The FD's role in this process could be critical. The FD manages the cash flow and working capital, including payment of creditors. What is the point of the production line being set up to produce maximum efficiency if the supplies do not arrive on time? The consequent loss of production, credibility or even customers may greatly outweigh the short term financial saving in the longer term. More and more companies will move towards preferred supplier management, even going as far as involving the suppliers in an understanding of their corporate plans, so that they feel part of the company.

Government and regulation

Very few organisations have no relationship with government departments, regulators, etc. (leaving aside the Inland Revenue and Customs and Excise). All companies must file annual returns and accounts with Companies House. In the financial services industry, there is a plethora of regulators. Companies must keep in mind the requirements of the Stock Exchange. Relationships such as these can of course be managed passively (until a problem occurs). It has been found that proactively managing relationships with regulators and other authorities can be particularly beneficial in terms of how an organisation is viewed or treated. Aggression certainly does not help.

The FD may often combine the role of company secretary, in which case the aforementioned is even more pertinent. FDs will also often be the lead role for liaison with external auditors and inspectors (where relevant). For these and all similar relationships, the general comments made previously are pertinent. Managing key relationships will be just one of the differentiators of outstanding organisations in the future. Look at the way commercial suppliers of services are managing relationships with your organisation and the money they are prepared to invest, including corporate hospitality, customer visits, etc.

Financiers

As with shareholders, any supplier of finance to the company requires careful and considerate management (including potential suppliers of capital). These may include bankers, venture capitalists, leasing companies, etc. Increasingly in the 1990s the focus has been on partnerships and strategic alliances. Creating a relationship which feels like a partnership, but without the legal standing, can still be long lasting and deliver commensurate benefits. Any time invested in developing and sustaining such relationships is justified.

The public

The public can be the number one enemy of a company. This can have long term devastating effects. Look at the way that the public has changed company policies and practices in, for example, the area of the environment. Production and use of CFCs was changed much faster by public boycott of aerosols than by government policy. Union Carbide felt a reaction in the UK to plans to establish a production plant due to the worldwide publicity of the Bhopal incident – not just the event itself, but also the way the public perceived the company's handling of it. British Midland's corporate reputation soared as a result of the East Midlands disaster simply because of the skilful and open way that management handled it in the media. It goes without saying that any FD who is likely to be involved with the public, media, analysts, etc. would benefit from media and PR management skills.

Employees

Finally, but by no means least, the FD must be skilled not only in handling his or her own managers and staff, but also anyone else at any level in the company. Increasingly, companies will look for managers with strong interpersonal and team management skills, capable of working at and dealing with all levels in a company. As more and more people feel empowered within organisations, the FD will need to be more approachable and come out of the ivory tower. Plain speaking, presentation skills and of course the ability to talk and negotiate easily with staff representatives will be fundamental to the team playing FD of the future.

> The art of effective listening is essential to clear communication, and clear communication is necessary to management success. Since the biggest part of your job as an executive consists in getting things done through people, it will pay you to learn how to become a good listener if you aren't one already. (J C Penney).

16

The FD as quality manager

In the future world, only quality organisations should be allowed to survive. Only visionary, adaptable, change oriented organisations should thrive. While this is as relevant to the FD as to anyone else in the organisation, it may provide a greater challenge to finance people than some others. In many organisations of various different kinds, the finance department has traditionally held a monitoring, reporting and controlling role. The organisation of tomorrow will need to be assured that controls are in place in the context of corporate governance or regulation, but the role of FD must become much more one of facilitating, advising and supporting.

TQM

In any competitive economy, continuous cost reduction and quality improvement are essential if an organisation is to stay in operation. Competitiveness is measured by three things: quality, price and delivery. The theory behind the costs of quality shows that, as quality improves, costs fall through reduction in failure and appraisal costs. Satisfying the customer in terms of quality *and* price will clearly benefit market share. The absence of quality problems also removes the need for the 'hidden operations' devoted to dealing with failure and waste, and delivery performance benefits from increased output and higher productivity. We cannot avoid seeing how quality has developed into the most important competitive weapon, and many organisations have realised that total quality management (TQM) is the new way of managing for the future. TQM is far wider in its application than assuring product or service quality – it is a way of managing the whole business or organisation to ensure complete customer satisfaction at every stage, internally and externally. (Oakland, 1989).

Oakland structures his approach around twelve words:

- Understanding
- Organisation
- Planning
- System
- Control
- Training

- Commitment
- Measurement
- Design
- Capability
- Teamwork
- Implementation

The only key word which seems to be missing from this list is process. Oakland connotes this in system. It is the processes, and the systems which support them, which represent how the organisation spends the money. Re-engineering has been much in vogue recently, mainly as a way of cutting costs. As suggested earlier, the organisation should keep under constant review what processes are necessary to deliver and sustain the strategy. An activity based management approach starts from this premise. A standard costing based approach can actually inhibit the potential cost efficiency arising from a quality management approach, for example, if capacity management is practised, rather than inventory management. If the right decisions are made, there should be no need to cut costs, as opposed to saving money through quality processes.

The finance department of tomorrow will plan and manage everything through a TQM type approach. This would start with an audit of every financial process or system and an inventory of the collective competencies available. These would then be compared with the processes, systems and competencies necessary to deliver the longer term strategic plan and the shorter term business plan while remaining flexible and adaptable to change. Multiskilling will become increasingly important to all departments of the organisation. The finance department will be no exception. People will develop competencies by sideways moves into different roles whereby they can not only acquire the wider skills to support the organisation, but also to progress towards the FD's post or even into broader general management roles. To do so, they will spend time in or working with other departments and also acquiring a portfolio of management skills.

Targets and quality costs

Dr W Edwards Deming is generally regarded as the father of quality management. Among his 14 Points for Management are:

- end the practice of awarding business solely on the basis of price tag;
- eliminate work standards that prescribe numerical quotas for the workforce and numerical goals for people in management;
- clearly define top management's permanent commitment to ever improving quality and productivity.

(Deming, 1989).

These give much for the FD to think about. Quality is as important as price, because it is total cost which matters, not initial cost (the goods may be cheap but what is the return and repair rate). Numerical targets can be counterproductive. Overachievement can lead to relaxation, complacency and loss of momentum. Overambitious targets can lead to demotivation. If targets are to be set they should be kept under constant review by the team. Management should cycle through a process of plan, implement, measure, review, improve. To that could be added innovate. The challenges are growing and never ending.

> Costs are inevitably incurred ensuring that products or services meet the customer's requirements. These are the quality related costs. An understanding of quality related costs is essential for any business. The costs associated with the mismanagement of quality (the costs of non-conformance) are often large; are non-productive; and are avoidable through the implementation of TQM. Quality costs can amount to twenty-five per cent of turnover. (Munro-Faure, 1992).

The importance of the FD understanding the concept of quality costs is self-evident. Continuous review of performance and the business processes will provide plenty of evidence for opportunities to improve. If the teams are empowered, they will both discover and implement the improvements – and share in the rewards. This will help to motivate a constant search for quality. This quality is not just an end in itself, however. The supply side view is related to a move towards perfection of the product. The demand side would focus on perfecting the satisfaction of the customers' needs and changing requirements. For both the producer and the consumer, the never ending focus should be on quality and value for money. Margins will remain under pressure unless volumes can be sustained or grown and productivity continually improved. The key to the latter is TQM. There is no better place for the FD to start than in the finance function. As an overhead, finance must understand and meet its internal customers' needs and constantly improve the quality, efficiency and 'fit' of its processes.

> Where quality fails or optimum quality is not achieved, there are quality costs. 'The costs of quality are no different from any other costs in that, like the costs of maintenance, design, sales, production, and other activities, they can be budgeted, measured and analysed.' (Oakland, 1989).

Oakland categorises four types of quality cost:

- internal and external failure costs;
- appraisal costs;
- prevention costs.

In 1996, the FD of Shorts of Belfast estimated that his business profits could be doubled by eradicating the costs of poor quality. Professor Juran has defined quality costs as 'the sum of costs that would disappear if there were no quality problems.' Some people would ask whether you need to measure quality costs or not. In this country, the answer is probably yes, for a number of reasons. First, we have tended to take a somewhat mechanistic approach to quality management in the UK. One way to convince management that such an approach is warranted is by calculating how much is being lost in quality costs. Second, the dedication to quality management has slipped in recent years. Many organisations could demonstrate that this is a lost opportunity and prove to themselves that standards have slipped, but lost customers, sales and profits are every bit as significant as higher costs. What we have failed to do, with few exceptions, is to absorb the Japanese (indeed Far Eastern) culture, where quality is everything, satisfied customers and sound profits are the result. There, the focus is on zero defects and therefore quality costs are an irrelevance.

Optimising performance and quality may involve culture changes for the finance department as well. By and large, manufacturing organisations are still inventory and standard costing led. Not surprisingly, a prime focus may be to reduce manufacturing costs. Unit cost can be reduced by producing more, especially by large batch runs, but you can end up with substantial inventories. If, on the other hand, you move to a capacity management basis, coupled with JIT, there is likely to be spare capacity in machines and labour. Standard costing would show a woeful picture and ABC would be more appropriate. Indeed from any point of view, ABC, ABCM, ABM, etc. are preferable to traditional management and costing methods.

As far as the FD is concerned from a management accounting perspective, this means changing from a departmental and product based focus, to process and customer orientation. If the organisation is to be totally quality and customer focused, then both the methods and the culture of the finance department must accord, otherwise management will question its commitment, if not its contribution or even relevance in this respect. One area of quality cost is inefficient, ineffective or redundant processes.

Engineering the processes and quality standards

Engineering the processes should be ongoing in response to change and innovation. The organisation should cycle through continuous improvement. The FD would be expected to support this approach as a member of the team and lead it in the finance function. Constantly redetermining the processes which are needed to deliver the strategy will result in changes in the pattern of costs as redundant activities cease and new ones are added. Cutting costs should not need to be an end in itself unless the organisation is in trouble. If it is any more than a short term expedient to buy the time to review strategy and implementation then the medium term outlook would be bleak.

Process re-engineering may have become almost as hackneyed as TQM and BS5750 (now rationalised into the international ISO 9000 series). Fundamentally, however, all of these approaches are sound as long as they are not seen in isolation from the overall pursuit of quality and continuous improvement, or done as one-off exercises. The important things are the principles and intentions and the desired outcome. It may be easier to think one's way through the introduction of quality management by considering fundamental concepts. For example:

- Total quality means understanding and meeting customers' needs first time every time. In the quality organisation the whole marketing philosophy is directed towards this objective. Everyone and every process faces the customer. Treating each other as customers helps, thinking as a customer helps.

- Process re-engineering is all about re-engineering every single process into a coherent whole to deliver the quality objective. It means, in the context of meeting customers' needs, asking oneself the question 'with what I now know, if I was designing this organisation from scratch, how would I engineer the processes (and the supporting systems) in order to meet those needs'. It also means dispensing with processes or intermediate steps which add no value or inhibit the overall purpose.

In tomorrow's world, such processes will be an unaffordable luxury. The only exception will be those processes which enable the organisation to research, design, develop and evolve to keep pace with the change in the market place and the immediate environment. It means being prepared for constant change, adapting like an evolving organism.

BS5750 was useful to organisations wishing to build clearly defined, checkable quality standards. Unfortunately, it tended to become an end in itself, rather than one means towards a quality organisation. Benchmarking of all kinds is just as valuable. BS5750 may have helped an organisation to get or keep customers (even being used as a mandatory hurdle for getting business in the public sector), but it is not sufficient in itself. ISO 9001 has achieved even more widespread acceptance (some say in seventy per cent of companies). As an approach it might appeal to the FD, but what is really needed is the continuous cycle of improvement referred to earlier, with everyone empowered to contribute to the evolving success of the department/organisation. On its own, ISO9001 or BS5750 did not prove that. Indeed they have been characteristically augmented by Investors In People or other standards, such as EFQM.

Some may say that SMEs would find it hard to follow this route. In *Insider* (February 1998), John Downie of the Federation of Small Businesses was quoted as saying 'I think the majority of small businesses are still fairly suspicious and cynical of the whole thing. While I believe that the principles are good for small businesses, actually going through the whole process within the timescale I don't think is worth it. It's a hell of a route to go through, and people seem to do it, I think, not for the practical reasons. They seem to do it to get on tender lists and be an approved company. A lot of times while they're going through it they're not actually taking it in and believing it.'

If you want to look on everything in terms of the costs to be saved and the technical quality of product, you can, if you are diligent, achieve material gains in profitability. If you wish to achieve lasting gains, however, you need a holistic approach to the strategy, management, risks, people, processes and systems which are the essence of your corporate being. ISO9001, or IIP, may get you a contract, or only the right to bid, but what happens if your processes and systems let you down in delivery? The world is undergoing dramatic, ongoing change. Global markets are still shaping themselves. Technology and a total quality approach to people and processes can now get a new player well into the game. Look at the production facilities which have moved to former third world countries. This is not always based on cheap labour alone. Quality is an attitude of mind and many questions flow from this.

Benchmarking

One of the most recent developments in the general area of quality management is benchmarking. We may set internal standards of performance which are 'stretching but achievable' but how do we know we are doing as well as we can? One way is to measure our performance against our peers. Here is an area where the FD can take a lead. As I said earlier, there is no world-class UK organisation, in quality terms. Indeed many are slipping away from the mark rather than approaching it. Having discussed specific performance measures in an earlier chapter, I will restrict myself to a more general context here.

Benchmarking is a growing practice. For a long time, organisations were too parochial to use such an approach. Anonymity is helpful when there is close competition and often an intermediary, such as a consultant, can be used to collect the data confidentially, for interfirm comparison. Benchmarking need not necessarily be limited to a particular industry or sector. The purpose is to compare, question and improve.

Businesses need to understand the skills and processes which are the keys to their success and to satisfying the requirements of their customers. Benchmarking can provide management with the necessary data to enable them to review critically their performance in these key areas against the best in the world....Benchmarking provides an insight into what is possible; an understanding of how it can be achieved; and a goal to aim for and exceed. (Munro-Faure, 1992).

Quality and the finance department

The FD has the task of leading all of the above in the finance department. Also, he or she will consciously or unconsciously impact the development of quality management elsewhere in the organisation. As suppliers to everyone in the organisation, the finance department could unwittingly set a bad example to the rest of the organisation by setting or delivering standards of quality below those elsewhere. Also, by indicating a reluctance to adapt, the FD can not only damage the reputation of the finance department but also immediate career prospects. The FD must be able to move on quality at least at the pace of other members of the corporate team by virtue of leading the key internal support function. This would be even more the case if the FD also had responsibility for information systems. They too must adapt to support the quality based development of the organisation.

The concept of striving for excellence has become a little overtaken by managing for change. Every organisation should now include within its overall strategy the drive to become a total quality organisation. Leading that process will be no less a challenge for the FD than any other member of the management team.

Who will survive? Companies that adopt constancy of purpose for quality, productivity and service, and go about it with intelligence and perseverance, have a chance to survive. (Deming, 1986).

17

The FD as a professional

> Objectivity, independence and intellectual honesty are personal qualities which are needed in order that (the FD) can give management a clear and unbiased view of financial performance and of investment/disinvestment decisions. (Sir William Purves, 1995, Group Chairman, HSBC Holdings plc).

Whatever else they become and whatever challenges they face in the changing organisation of the future, every FD will be expected to remain above all a professional in every aspect of the role.

The FD's role often combines other professional functions, sometimes led by and sometimes possessed by the FD. It is not unknown to find a finance director with two or more qualifications: accountant and solicitor; accountant and company secretary; accountant and corporate treasurer; etc. The FD does not need more than one qualification in order to manage a broad function. However, it is increasingly attractive to consider the relevance of a broad business qualification, such as an MBA. What FDs will always need are the competence, the managerial skills and the understanding sufficient to ask the right questions and retain the respect and leadership of a multidisciplinary team. Such skills and the right personal and interpersonal skills will be good grounding for the next step up.

In *The Changing Role of the Finance Director* (the report referred to in Chapter 2), 'Supporters of the chartered accountant route tended to put a high premium on monitoring and control skills. The relative inadequacy of MBAs in this area, some commented, makes it dangerous to rely on this source for future finance directors.' However, 'unless the training changes, (said one senior FD) chairmen, chief executives and recruitment consultants will decide that the key aspects of the job are more closely matched by other qualifications; finance directors will have accountants working for them in the same way as tax or treasury specialists, but the high ground will have been lost to MBAs.'

> The greater part of the finance director's contribution will be to the future of the business through strategic planning, corporate planning and financial structuring. In these roles, it is hard to avoid the conclusion that an MBA may be an equally valuable qualification as accountancy. (David Timson, 1995).

Ethics

> The key aspects of a FD's job for me (include) ensuring that the company operates in a tightly controlled and ethical environment. (Chief Executive, 1995, electricity company).

> I passionately hold ethics high on my list because ethics moderates power and directs it for good. (Steve Shirley, 1995, Life President, FI Systems Group).

The Institute of Business Ethics provides a model statement and code as a possible framework for organisations to develop their own. It does not recommend simply copying from someone else. Ethics are very much a part of current business life and will remain so. They will increasingly be a reflection of the public's view of how organisations should conduct themselves, combined with that organisation's own standards. They will become an inextricable part of the corporate brand. If an organisation is seen to be operating unethically in any part of its daily activities, e.g. how it treats customers and employees, how it deals with the environment, advertising standards, behaviour of its top people, etc., the brand and image may be damaged. The experience of British Gas showed that, together with other privatised companies.

Accountants are of course expected to operate to the highest professional and ethical standards. The disciplinary procedures for chartered accountants for example are correctly strict in this respect (as for most professions). FDs therefore should also act professionally and ethically. With their governance and director's hats on they will be closely involved in the process and consideration. Cadbury encouraged the development of codes of ethics. In the US, ethics codes have not only mitigated penalties for offences such as fraud, but have improved employees' views of company behaviour.

The consummate professional will not only be expected to display high standards in his or her own discipline, but also in general. If FDs cannot be relied on to set and observe high ethical and personal standards, values and beliefs, it must start to undermine the credibility and reputation both of the FDs and the company they serve. Any suggestion or proof that the organisation has fallen short in this respect will adversely affect customer preference. There has been a middle class backlash against greed and abasement of standards. The finance director will be expected no less than the managing director or the chairman of the organisation to display and indeed champion those corporate and personal ethics, standards and values.

18

The shape of things to come

> 'Change' is scientific, 'progress' is ethical. Change is indubitable, whereas progress is a matter of controversy. (Bernard Russell).

There are more accountants per capita in the UK than any other country in the world. Some will say that the influence of accountants in industry has inhibited the progress of British industry since the last war. Accountants have not always in the past been adaptable to change. Many of the leading business people approached for help with this book not only pointed to the widening role of the FD, but also questioned whether broader qualifications would not be appropriate to the FD's role in future, e.g. MBA and ACT. My own view is that the role and functions of the FD have grown and changed so much in the last ten to twenty years that it is time to consider a qualification specific to the FD's role. The content might well cover all the areas addressed in this text.

Successful organisations will increasingly in future be led by empowering, creative, adaptable, entrepreneurial, caring, visionary leaders. The FD's role will need to move in this direction also. The finance function cannot be a check on the business, it should facilitate, advise, guide and support. The globalisation of economies is leading to the most intense competitiveness. The UK will need to be highly adaptable to survive, let alone thrive. As a nation we have been famed in the past for our inventive genius and industrial leadership. We still retain a relatively stable political and social environment. We have the opportunities to draw on all the wonderful talents of our people to succeed if we show good empowering leadership. FDs can be in the van of this change or they can follow it. To lead it they will need to draw on all the skills discussed in this report and be able to work strongly in teams based on collective understanding and purpose.

In 'Careers Without Ladders' (*Accountancy*, October 1994) Robert Bruce reflected on the dramatic consequences of the recession:

> But two things have changed in management. First, the recession has completely upended views on the quality of leader a company needs. Second, young managers' aspirations have been radically changed by the experience of the great late-1980s business boom. The recession hit companies that would normally be able to ride out such setbacks. The quality of management was cruelly exposed. Anyone, particularly accountants, can adopt the approach of cutting back to adapt to lower demand. That's fine if the recession is a blip. Instead, it was an almighty bump. The management qualities required were vision, rapid change and leadership. And these qualities are not usually associated with people from an accounting background. (Bruce, 1994).

Conclusions

So what....about the make-up of the future finance director. If the stereotypical picture of the group finance director of years gone by is of a very solid chartered accountant, a tough controller with his finger on the financial accounts, many years – possibly a whole career in the same company; the paradigm for the future may be that of an internationalist who has worked in several countries and in several different industries on his or her way to the top. They will probably still be a qualified accountant, but will be likely to also have an MBA or a tertiary qualification with the focus on financial risk and corporate finance. Their role will be as much that of strategist and general manager as 'numbers person.' And finally, they will be obliged to have current and sophisticated risk management experience. (David Timson, 1995).

The world is changing, but not as rapidly in all respects. Is this good news or bad news? Many of the things written in the mid 1980s are still valid today, ten years later – even in technology. Quality management has been one of the greatest influences on management philosophy in the last decade, but Deming was advising the Japanese on it in the 1950s. Much modern management thinking captures ideas that have been around for decades, but which did not have wide appeal or credibility before. Now we live in an environment of constant change and chaos – but we always did! Much which I wrote in the first edition of this book has already come to pass, or is out of date. If this edition reads like a new text, that is what it has felt like at times. The journey of writing it has been even more exciting and inspiring than the first time, despite the huge challenges and potential disasters which now stare us in the face. They will undoubtedly prove to be just as much of an opportunity to some as they are a terminal threat to others.

We may worry about how our children can cope with the present world but our parents worried about the same. The human being is incredibly adaptable. We see this change through our eyes, but we are not adapting as fast as our children – and yet we have the capacity to do so. Several years ago, I travelled on the QE2 to New York in November. For five days, we had to find ways to amuse ourselves. The IBM PC had recently been produced. There was a lab equipped with a dozen on board ship. No matter what time I tried, I could not get onto them, because they were always being used by people well past their pension. It opened my eyes. Now we live in that world.

And as for chaos – it is not new, only the theory is. An increasing number of people are acknowledging that we cannot explain everything. It is no longer macho to trumpet one logic against another. We now look to quantum physics to explain everything. Surprise, challenge, contra-indication, etc. have always been the order of the day. Do we bemoan the fact or do we grasp the opportunity? Finance is changing – that is an opportunity.

Not long after writing *Thriving on Chaos* Tom Peters wrote in *Liberation Management*:

> While less successful business people retain consulting chaoticians to construct ponderous models aimed at explaining what went wrong yesterday, the champion entrepreneur gets in another ten tries, one of which just might click. (Peters, 1993).

In *The Change Masters*, Rosabeth Moss Kanter wrote:

> The ultimate skill for change mastery works on just that larger context surrounding the innovation process. It consists of the ability to conceive, construct, and convert into behaviour a new view of organisational reality. (Kanter, 1985).

So let us get on with it.

I am attracted to the view that an organisation while constantly reviewing its environment and recognising the community in which it exists must operate on the basis of always knowing what its customers need and producing the highest affordable quality to meet that need precisely, while determining what is best for its stakeholders – its shareholders, sponsors, donors, etc., and most of all its own people. Maslow and Herzberg did not have all the answers and nor did Kotler, Porter or Peters but all of these and many more have a share in the understanding of what is right for your organisation, your customers and your people.

And what of the FD? Read all that you want but never follow it slavishly unless it is the law, or ethical or professional good practice. My own approach has been to acquire information and then put it on one side; to seek to learn and understand the organisation, its people, its industry or sector and its environment and then to let the natural conclusions evolve as to how best to proceed. Good, sound modern management theory and practice are essential to that understanding but nothing can replace the understanding of the people and their needs, the key importance of information and the paramount importance of quality in every action.

No FD is an island. We may have been allowed to act in such a way in the past, but the modern FD understands, empowers, facilitates and leads by example. Control and sound financial management are still fundamental but they should be by the organisation for the organisation, facilitated by an FD who is both a professional and truly a general manager as well as being the most numerate and objective strategist in the organisation.

What will bond successful organisations in future will be:

- brand and capital (critical investment factors);

- leadership;

- values and team spirit;

- common beliefs and practices;

- complementary needs;

- geography;

- technology;

- mutual contracts.

As I write this last chapter, year 2000 is a daily topic of conversation. By the time you read my words, I do hope they are relevant only as a source of great challenge and opportunity, on the verge of a golden era of prosperity and a century where art, knowledge and the right brain will at last allow us to capitalise holistically on the astonishing scientific achievements of the 20th century.

> Keep constantly in mind in how many things you yourself have witnessed change already. The universe is change, life is understanding. (Marcus Aurelius).

Bibliography

Alder, H. (1993) *The Right Brain Manager*, Judy Piatkus Publishers Ltd.

Armstrong, M. (1997) *Management Processes and Functions*, IPM.

Armstrong, M. (Ed.) (1990) *The New Managers Handbook*, Kogan Page.

Association of Corporate Treasurers (1995/96 and annually) *The Treasurer's Handbook.*

Association of Corporate Treasurers (1995) *Derivatives for Directors.*

Association of Corporate Treasurers (1994) *Risk Management and Control of Derivatives.*

Association of Corporate Treasurers (1997) *Uses of Derivatives.*

Auditing Practices Board (1994) *Internal Financial Control Effectiveness.*

Chaudry-Lawton & Lawton (1992) *Ignition*, BCA.

The Committee on the Financial Aspects of Corporate Governance (1992) *The Financial Aspects of Corporate Governance*, Gee and Co.

Deming, W.E. (1989) *Deming's 14 Points for Management*, British Deming Association.

Deming, W.E. (1986) *Out of the Crisis*, Massachusetts Institute of Technology, Center for Advanced Engineering Study.

Drucker, P.F. (1990) *Managing the Non-Profit Organisation*, Butterworth-Heinemann.

Drucker, P.F. (1992) *Managing for the Future*, Butterworth-Heinemann.

Egan, G. *Re-engineering the Company Culture*, Egan/Hall Partnership. (Out of print).

Financial Executives Group of the Board for Chartered Accountants in Business (1993) *The Changing Role of the Finance Director.*

Goldratt, E. (1984) *The Goal*, Gower Press.

Goldratt, E. (1986) *The Race*, Gower Press.

Hammer and Champy (1994) *Reengineering the Corporation*, Nicholas Brealey Publishing.

Handy, C. (1989) *The Age of Unreason*, Century Business.

Handy, C. (1994) *The Empty Raincoat*, BCA

Jacobs, D. (1991) *Making Your Business Competitive*, Kogan Page.

Kanter, R.M. (1985) *The Change Masters*, Unwin Hyman Limited.

Lipsey, R.G. (1963) *Positive Economics*, Weidenfeld & Nicolson.

Loose, P. and Yelland, J. (1987) *The Company Director*, Jordan & Sons Limited.

Mintzberg, H. (1973) *The Nature of Managerial Work*, New York, Harper & Row.

Munro-Faure, L. and M. (1992) *Implementing Total Quality Management*, Financial Times Pitman Publishing.

Oakland, J.S. (1989) *Total Quality Management*, Heinemann Professional Publishing.

Owen, G. and Abel, P. (1993) *The Changing Role of the Finance Director*, Finance Executives Group of the Board for Chartered Accountants in Business of the Institute of Chartered Accountants in England and Wales.

Parker, D. and Stacey, R. (1994) *Chaos, Management and Economics: the Implications of Non-Linear Thinking*, IEA.

Peters, T. (1993) *Liberation Management*, Pan Books Ltd.

Peters, T. (1987) *Thriving on Chaos*, Pan Books Ltd.

Pike, R. and Dobbins, R. (1986), *Investment Decisions and Financial Strategy*, Philip Alan Publishers Limited.

Price Waterhouse (1997) *CFO Architect of the Corporation's Future*, Wiley.

Price Waterhouse (1997) *In Search of Shareholder Value*, Pitman Publishing

RSA, (1995) *Tomorrow's Company*, Royal Society for the Encouragement of Arts, Manufacturers and Commerce.

Sarch, Y. (1991) *How to be Headhunted*, Business Books Ltd.

Stacey, R. (1994) *Dynamic Management and Scientific Chaos*, Kogan Page.

Stacey, R. (1994) *Dynamic Management for the 1990s*, Kogan Page.

Tromans, S. and Irvine, G. (1994) *Directors in the Dock*, Technical Communications (Publishing) Ltd.